SUNLIGHT AND STEEL

·······································

THE STORY OF
THE SS INDEPENDENCE AND THE SS CONSTITUTION

BY
STEWART GORDON AND WILLIAM MILLER

FEATURING
THE PHOTOGRAPHS OF BOB HARROW

BOOK DESIGN BY JOSEPH RADDING

PROW PRESS

ANN ARBOR, MICHIGAN

Published by   Prow Press
               PO Box 4190
               Ann Arbor, MI 48105

Edition #1

Library of Congress Catalog Number: 98-67568

ISBN: 0-9667165-0-7

This book is set in Skia, Stone Sans, Bank Gothic, and Swing.
Printed in the United States at Thomson-Shore, Inc., Dexter, Michigan.

SUNLIGHT & STEEL:
CONTENTS

This book began because an architect fell in love with a ship. In 1995, Al Luthmers, then Director of Development for American Hawaii Cruises, asked me to become historian/consultant for the recovery of the history of the *Independence*. He saw that the ship was much more than a way to get from island to island; it was one of the great achievements of American technology and design in the post-WWII period. Through almost a year, I searched archives, traced leads, and put out the call for interviews with former crew, passengers, and executives.

The results were extraordinary. There was an outpouring of affection for the ship and rich photo records from all periods of her history. Even within the company, there were unexpected treasures in old files. When the official project with American Hawaii ended, I remained fascinated with both the *Independence* and her sister ship the *Constitution*, and continued the research.

My first "goldmine" was my initial interview with Bob Harrow. Bob was the onboard photographer from the ships' earliest years. His firm took the photos on both ships, and Bob was regularly aboard. He "shot" the humble and the famous, from tourist class to Grace Kelly.

He also kept enough of his work to give an unprecedented image of the ship, its workings, and its famous clientele in the 1950's and 1960's. I am proud to have Bob Harrow's unique work in this book, and his help throughout the project.

To put the ships in their proper context, I needed a great ocean liner historian; my collaborator, William Miller, is one of the premier liner historians in the world. He is the author of more than forty books on liners, and has delivered countless lectures both on and off ships. He brings a depth of research and a passion which you will find all through the book.

The many interviews and personal photos make this book much more than the story of two ships. It is the story of the people who envisioned them, toiled to build them, worked on their decks and in their engine rooms, sat at dinner as passengers, and boarded them to come to America. All who sail on the ship share in that tradition; so do those who appreciate and come to understand the *Independence* and the *Constitution*.

Stewart Gordon
Ann Arbor, Michigan

CHAPTER ONE:
THE PRINCESS & THE PRINCE

On April 4, 1956, the *Constitution*, in New York harbor, was the site of much more world wide attention than she had received at her launch, five years earlier. Four thousand writers and reporters tried to book passage. Spectators jammed the pier and every available vantage point. Everyone waited to be part of a fairy tale come true. Grace Kelly and her wedding party boarded; she was about to become a real American princess, crossing the Atlantic to marry Prince Rainier of Monaco.

The story started more than a year earlier. Grace Kelly, the daughter of a self-made millionaire from Philadelphia, was at the peak of a successful acting career, one of the most beautiful and desirable women in the world. Prince Rainier was the lonely monarch of a tiny state in southern France, home to 27,000 subjects and the profitable Monte Carlo casino. Popular myth, reinforced by the press, was that if Rainier did not produce an heir, Monaco would become simply another prefecture of France while the ancient, ruling Grimaldi line would come to an end. The romance had all of the unlikely, improbable elements which people wanted to believe could come true: the beautiful princess from the democracy would rescue the lonely prince and save his house from extinction.

Grace and Her Parents Board The Constitution

The story is both more complicated and more simple than the fairy tale. Grace Kelly's fans knew her from a string of hit movies - *High Noon* with Gary Cooper, *Mogambo* with Clark Gable, and *The Bridges of Toko-Ri*. Alfred Hitchcock found in her a perfect combination of Nordic beauty and suppressed passion and cast her in *Rear Window, Dial M for Murder,* and *To Catch A Thief.* In 1953, her face was featured on the cover of *Life* magazine and, in 1955, Grace won the Academy Award for Best Actress for *The Country Girl.* She was no fairy princess locked away in a castle. Grace Kelly had a series of romances, some serious,

Footage for a Waiting Audience

from her late teenage years to her mid-twenties. These affairs included fellow actors and at least two male leads of her films. In 1954, she nearly married the twice-divorced fashion designer Oleg Cassini. Throughout her acting career, Grace Kelly showed the world a cool beautiful face, while maintaining strong focus in her acting and negotiating. Yet she displayed an unexpected playful abandon among close friends. The photos of Howell Conant, shot in Jamaica, captured her in this mood for a feature in *Colliers* magazine: Grace radiantly rising from the water with a look fresh and at the same time provocative.

In the first half of the 1950's, while Grace Kelly was becoming a star, Prince Rainier moved in European playboy circles. In 1955, he was already thirty one, and had ended a long affair. His occupations were those of royalty. He collected wild animals (for his zoo) and sports cars, took trips on the royal yacht, played golf, and gave state dinners, but he needed an heir. Investors in the banks and the casino felt that a pretty, young wife would add luster to the rather faded image of the principality.

The two met when journalist Pierre Galante arranged a photo shoot with Prince Rainier on his palace grounds for Grace Kelly, who headed the American film delegation at the 1955 Cannes Film festival. Much went badly; as the electricity was off at Kelly's hotel, she could not dry her hair or have the dress she wanted pressed. The Prince was late and the photo session shortened because Kelly had to return to Cannes for an evening event. Still, something happened in the short walk they took together viewing his animal collection and gardens. This was the start of a romance which captivated the world by the end of the year. Through that summer Grace was still deeply involved with Jean-Pierre Aumont, the French actor; the affair faded when she returned to America.

The Press Anxiously Awaits

None of the gossip columns found out about a correspondence between Grace and the Prince which continued throughout the summer and into the fall. Letters revealed the shy prince in a way which conversation had not, and gave the two a private space impossible for such public figures. Her movie of that summer was *The Swan,* a story about a woman deciding whether to marry a prince; it had uncanny parallels to her real life. When the film finished shooting in December, Grace headed back to Philadelphia for the Kelly family Christmas. The family was informed that Prince Rainier would be in the United States for "medical" reasons and requested a social call during the holiday season. In reality, he was looking for a wife; the French government and even the Paris press knew it. His list included Grace Kelly. What began as a social call on Christmas day, 1955, progressed to amiable conversation between Grace's father and Father Tucker, an Irish priest and confidante of the prince, followed by intimate conversation between Prince Rainier and Grace. The next day, they went driving together; later in the day, the Prince proposed marriage.

For the fans and the rest of the world, the magic began in early January with a press conference at the Kelly's Philadelphia home. The engaged couple responded to questions - intelligent, obvious, and stupid. The fairy tale themes were established early, and built through the ensuing months. There was the worldly but lonely prince, and the virginal but beautiful princess-to-be. There seemed to be a unified effort to forget all of her previous lovers; from *Colliers* to *Good Housekeeping*, from *Time* to *Look,* every piece gushed. The only exception was a ten-part series by Grace's mother in all the Hearst papers which documented Grace's gawky teenage years and most of her romances, though not always by name.

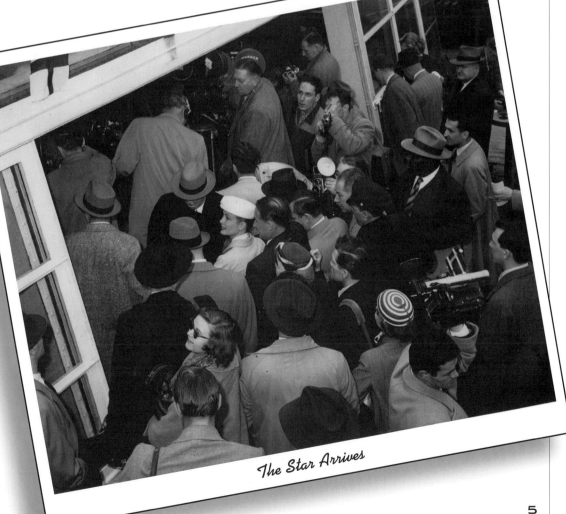

The Star Arrives

Nevertheless, the overall theme of even this series was the role of the Kelly parents in guiding Grace and breaking off these affairs before they went "too far".

Through the winter, the press pursued every angle - was the Prince good enough for an American film goddess (the Chicago papers thought not) and most pointedly, would Grace Kelly continue to make films. Still, most pieces on the engagement were wholly positive. It was a time when America valued being a wife and mother even above being a film star. Magazines like *Good Housekeeping* lived on the fantasy that even the most beautiful and famous women wanted first and foremost to be wives and mothers. The story had all the elements of hope, tenderness, and commitment. The fantasy was not that far off; Grace had seen most of her friends married. Several already had children. She saw marriage as the next natural phase in her life, and had always been determined to be in control of her life.

Unflappable Even in the Press Conference Madness

Through the winter and into the spring, Grace worked in Hollywood on what would be her last picture, *High Society*, with a host of singers - Frank Sinatra, Bing Crosby, and Louis Armstrong. While Grace worked on voice lessons to sing a duet with Bing Crosby, Prince Rainier became more direct with reporters that the role of film star was incompatible with that of princess of Monaco. Even MGM slowly accepted that Grace Kelly was moving into a public part that their contract could not control. They made the best of it and gave her a spectacular wedding dress, the services of her usual hair stylist for the wedding, and a substantial cash bonus.

From March until the actual wedding in May, Grace Kelly was at the center of a press frenzy, feeding an insatiably curious world. Reporters followed her everywhere. They photographed her buying clothes in New York. Reporters speculated about the food in Monaco, and they asked Grace about bridesmaids' dresses and the color of the socks of the royal guard. The *Daily Worker* groused that this daughter of a bricklayer had chosen someone who couldn't lay bricks. Family pictures of most of the Kellys and some of the Grimaldis found their way into *Colliers, Look, Time* and *Newsweek. Womenswear Daily* had a field day analyzing the "Grace Kelly look". NBC ran a two week series on the history and culture of Monaco. *Life* magazine ran a special set of cartoons gently caricaturing the wedding preparations in Monaco. The band wagon rolled merrily on. A bra and girdle manufacturer told his dealers to stock extra merchandise as he was planning day by day bulletins from Monaco. Many noticed that the wedding was the biggest non-political event since the coronation of Queen Elizabeth II. Through it all, Grace smiled, waved, answered questions and remained, well, gracious.

Lifeboat Drill — Stars and Poodles First

Sunlight on a Gray Day at Sea

Dressing Well for the Party

TAKEN ABOARD THE SUNLINERS
• SS CONSTITUTION
• SS INDEPENDENCE

AMERICAN
EXPORT LINES

The Navigation Lesson

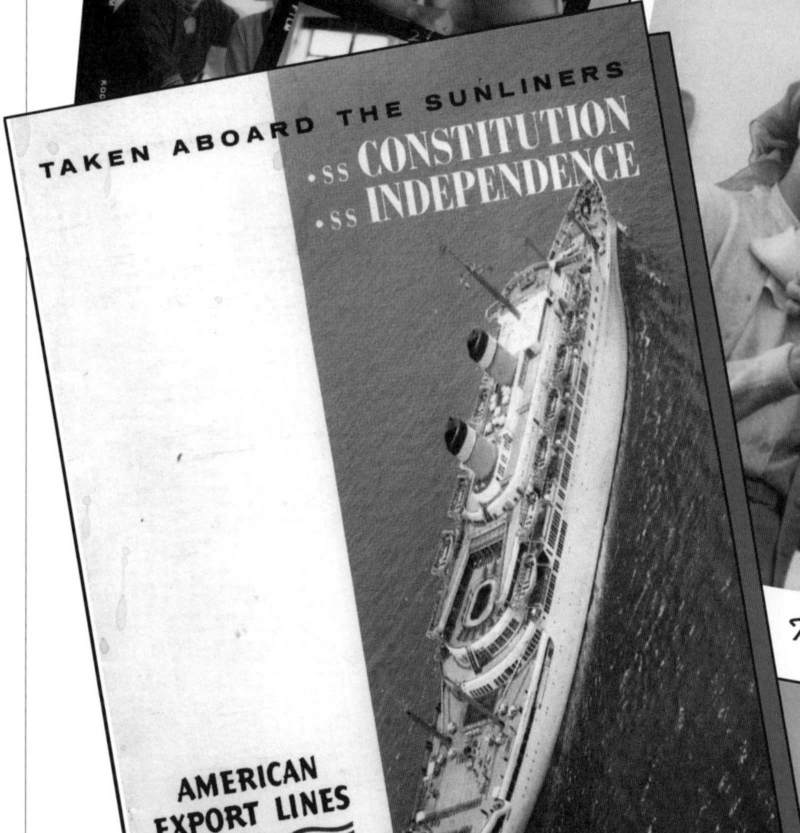

Photo Folder
"Taken Aboard the Constitution"

The Party Continues with Deck Games

The Photographer and His Willing Subject

Mid-Ocean, Grace Entertains Her Wedding Guests

Grace Kelly's involvement with the *Constitution* actually started years before the tumultuous send off in April. In 1950, Grace, barely twenty, was working both as a model and as a less-successful Broadway actress. One of her modeling assignments was the first promotional photos for the just-finished *Constitution.* Six years later, she had to decide how to take a large entourage to Europe for the wedding. She was supposed to fly on Air France, but American Export cleverly offered space on the *Constitution.* Cautious negotiations between the Kelly family and American Export Line began in early March. The Line saw the opportunity for great publicity; so did the Kellys. Initially, the two were far apart. Grace wanted free passage for a couple of hundred friends and family. American Export had already sold out the crossing. Gradually, compromises were worked out. Grace would travel with about ninety people and the Line would reschedule the displaced passengers. As the travel date approached, other issues cropped up. Grace wanted the crossing to be a private party, and pressured American Export to refuse booking any rooms to the press. When this failed, the Kelly family tried to confine the press to cabin class and deny them access to first class areas. All of this was impossible. More than 4000 news people tried to book passage; fans and well-wishers wanted coverage from the ship. The compromise put reporters in crowded bunks, often four to a room in cabin class, but allowed extremely limited access to first class areas. In addition, Grace would hold two large press conferences during the voyage.

Sailing day began with the arrival of the Grace's baggage - four steamer trunks, fifty six other pieces of baggage (including twenty hat boxes), and wedding presents ranging from a crated Queen Anne desk (from Cary Grant) to a Weimaraner puppy (from family friends in Philadelphia). Veteran ship reporters found the shipside scene the largest in a generation; it seemed like half of New York had come to wish Grace Kelly goodbye. The press conference around the pool was forced inside when it began to rain. A room designed to seat fifty people was packed with more than 200 reporters and photographers. They climbed on chairs, tables, and each other, and banged on the windows from outside when they could not get in, shouting questions. Bob Harrow, the shipboard photographer, by arrangement with Grace, popped up from a lifeboat and photographed the wall of press cameramen and reporters. This famous photo ran in *Life* magazine and was a favorite of Grace Kelly. After this riotous press conference, the ship, set to sail, was held up for more than forty five minutes as the crew tried to get well-wishers and press ashore. Finally, thousands of hands waved, confetti drifted down, cameras flashed, and the great ship left its pier. The waterfront had not seen an event like this since the first American boys returned from Europe after World War II. Though the *Constitution* sailed with the Kelly party, the country remained obsessed with the wedding. Ethel Merman starred in a quickly mounted Broadway play entitled *Happy Hunting*; the story line was a rich

Royal Yacht in Monaco Harbor

Philadelphia girl, snubbed by High Society, who was wooed and won by a Mediterranean nobleman.

Out in the Atlantic, the scene on the *Constitution* was anything but a normal crossing. Grace wanted the voyage to be like "summer camp", a time of play and fun with old friends and family. Unfortunately, there were more than a dozen rival journalists and photographers, all of whom had to generate stories. The first day at sea, Grace reported to her station for the required lifeboat drill and more than 250 passengers and all of the press arrived at the same station. The captain realized the futility of his efforts to move passengers to their proper stations and announced, "This lifeboat carries 150 people, but it looks like it's going to be crowded".

There were simply too many press for too few angles. Stories began to focus on the tiniest of events - the older generation sitting in a different area of the pool than the younger, leading to speculation of family discord - and had a generally sour tone. The Kelly family discussed the situation and decided to give some exclusive time to each of the journalists and photographers during the voyage, and the tone of the dispatches noticeably improved.

Watching the New York Skyline Recede

Each day, Grace spent several hours with practical matters in her cabin - paying bills, sorting papers, writing notes to those who had given her a party or a present. She also spent several hours with the press, walked both Oliver, her poodle, and the new Weimaraner puppy, and invited a few friends for tea and talk and discussion of arrangements. The crossing was relatively calm, with sunny skies and crisp April temperatures. The sixty six friends and family in the Kelly party retained the "summer camp" atmosphere. Every night had its incredibly rich dinners complete with toasts and speeches. After dinner, there were endless organized activities - dancing, party games, charades, canasta, bingo, pioneer sing-alongs, leaving America parties, and going to Europe parties.

Grace's Poodle at Home Under the Prince's Blanket

Substantial amounts of champagne were consumed. In mid-ocean, the *Constitution* passed its sister ship, the New York-bound *Independence,* which wired the message, "Good luck, Gracie". The last evening was subdued; everyone in the Kelly party was aware of moving out of the "summer camp" into a largely unknown European royal environment. Grace stayed in her stateroom; her sister, Peggy, gave her a manicure. Guests repacked their steamer trunks and suitcases.

Eight days after leaving New York, the *Constitution* made a special stop just outside Monaco harbor. The ship listed slightly to landward as all of the

A More Subdued Press Conference

Flowers from the King of Morocco

Quiet Conversation on Deck

Mr HARROW —
If you can get copies
of these, would you
be so kind as to send
them to:
S A S Princesse de Monaco
Palais Princier
Principauté de Monaco?

Bob Harrow
Gets a Royal Request

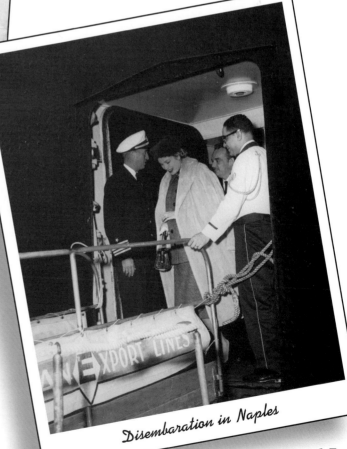

Disembaration in Naples

Very Much In Love

passengers crowded the rail of every deck. It was a gray and overcast day, but hundreds of small boats filled the harbor. At ten thirty, the white royal yacht left its pier, approached the *Constitution,* and placed a gangway from one vessel to the other. A helicopter dropped red and white carnations while Grace Kelly (carrying her poodle) left the *Constitution* and met Prince Rainier on the deck of the yacht. The rest of the wedding party followed by launch. At the dock awaited hundreds of press, hordes of girls with flags, several brass bands, and much cheering. Thus began a week of parties and receptions leading up to the wedding. The *Constitution* gave three great blasts of its whistle and departed for Genoa.

Only five months later, Grace Kelly was once again aboard the *Constitution,* returning to New York with Prince Rainier. The pomp of the royal wedding was behind them, as was the pleasant honeymoon on the royal yacht and the less pleasant infighting in the Grimaldi family. Many members openly snubbed Grace and the prospect of shopping in New York and seeing old friends must have been attractive. The voyage was much closer to an ordinary crossing - little press, no wedding entourage, fewer gawking passengers. Grace was just starting to show pregnancy; Caroline would be born four months later. In New York, Grace and Prince Rainier happily shopped Madison and Fifth Avenues for what turned out to be more than two tons of baby clothes and modern gadgets to spruce up the palace; evenings, they saw friends, and dined out. The press remained mesmerized; now, Grace Kelly was not only a real princess, but a mother-to-be. The interviews discussed morning sickness, baby clothes, and the like. Within a short time, the couple was back on the ship, returning to Monaco. Grace liked the onboard photographer, Bob Harrow, and permitted him to photograph the couple at leisure on the return voyage to Monaco - reading, walking on deck, talking, and playing cards. The couple was basking in the fulfillment of the need for an heir, and were clearly in love and very comfortable in each other's company. Grace, herself, asked for prints of some of the shots; the rest have remained with Bob Harrow as negatives for more than forty years and are published here for the first time.

The relationship between Grace Kelly and the *Constitution* continued for more than three decades; we shall return to a later episode of that story in Chapter Six.

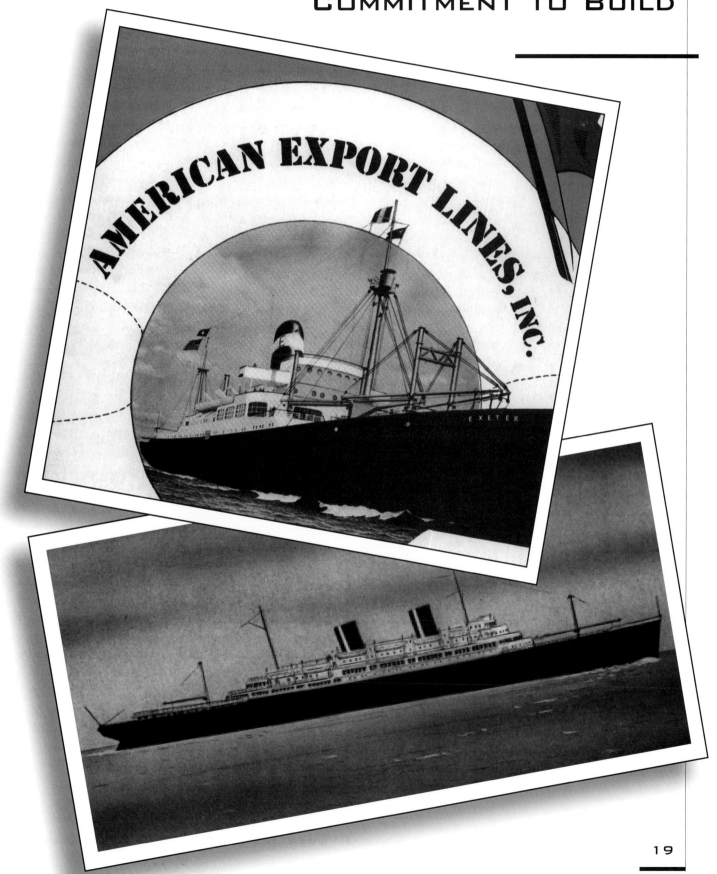

The story of the *Independence* and the *Constitution* began almost twenty years before the beautiful Grace Kelly waved goodbye to New York from the rail. If Grace had been on a luxurious transatlantic liner in 1936, rather than 1956, it would likely have been a foreign ship - British, Dutch, German, French, or even Scandinavian. Since she was bound for the Mediterranean, it would likely have been on an The Italian Line since they dominated this trade. Though the country was deep in the Depression, American shipping lines chaffed at this European dominance. They all recognized the profitable immigrant service from Europe to the United States as well as a strong tourist business to Europe. What brought dramatic change was a new Shipping Act of 1936 for which shipping lines and maritime and shipbuilding unions had lobbied hard. It offered government subsidies of approximately 50% of construction costs for passenger shipbuilding. Under this subsidy, the United States Lines quickly announced the 33,500 ton *America*, the largest US-built liner to date (completed in 1940). Within a few months, the Panama Railroad Company, another New York-based firm, announced construction of three superb, 216-passenger combination liners. Other firms jumped in. American President Lines revealed designs for Pacific passenger ships which they could convert to aircraft carriers; even the United Fruit Company planned new, high-speed passenger-carrying "banana boats".

One of the Pre-War "Four Aces"

American Export, though owner of a major freighter fleet, was - at that time - a minor player in the passenger field. The company owned only a quartet of 1931-built combination passenger-cargo ships named the *Excalibur*, the *Excambion*, the *Exeter*, and the *Exchorda*, known as the 'Four Aces". (These ships sailed at 85% passenger capacity throughout the middle 1930's and fueled expansionist thinking at the company).

Queen Elizabeth Ferrying Troops to Europe

In January 1938, American Export went public with its plans. While no actual specifications were released at the time, Export's technical department in Lower Manhattan drew up plans for three large (over 20,000 tons), fast (20 knots or better), and luxurious ships intended for the trans-Atlantic run to the Mediterranean. World War II was, however, rapidly approaching; the political and trade situation in Europe grew increasingly chaotic and most of America's planned ships were shelved. So, too, were American Export's three great liners.

During the War, officials in Washington were deeply impressed with the heroic, invaluable services of the Cunard liners, *Queen Mary* and *Queen Elizabeth*. Designed to carry some 2,000 passengers in peacetime, they were altered for War service with capacities of over 15,000 troops each. In October 1944, well before the War ended, and with the personal support of President Franklin D. Roosevelt, big, new American liners were very much under consideration. There was serious talk in the power chambers in Washington of launching a major federally-sponsored construction program of large passenger ships. Plans grew more concrete as well as more ambitious and were said

21

to include no less than eleven "superliners" for peacetime services around the world. With capacities of 1,500 to 2,000 passengers, they could be quickly converted to troop ships, if necessary. The first pair was intended for the North Atlantic run to England and France, or perhaps Holland or Germany.

In spite of continued pressure by the War Department, government enthusiasm for a major liner/troopship building program waned in 1946. By 1948, the original plans for eleven passenger ships dwindled to just six: for United States Lines, the giant *United States*, which at the time (1948) was estimated to be some 48,000 tons; twin 29,000-ton sister ships for the American Export Lines; and three smaller 13,000-ton combination passenger-cargo ships for American President Lines. The Government plan would directly subsidize more than half of the $150,000,000 cost to build these ships. Expectedly, there were those in Washington who were against such ships and in particular against their high costs. Nevertheless, the plan seemed a good balance at the time. The *United States* would serve Northern Europe; the two Export liners would sail to the Mediterranean; and the American President three-some —- *President Adams*, *President Jackson* and *President Hayes* —- would sail around the world. Through all of these discussions, American

Marine Flasher (Converted Troopship)

Export had a shipping line to run. During the War, three of the original "Four Aces" had been lost and the company sold the sole survivor, the *Exchorda*, to the Turkish Maritime Lines. Trying to get back into the passenger business, for a brief period the company ran two Italian liners, the *Saturnia* and the *Vulcania*, which had been seized by the US Government during the War and not yet officially released to their Italian Line owners.

"Just after the War, in 1945-46, American Export's Genoa office was strategic in the Company's passenger ship planning", recalls Herb Maletz, assistant comptroller at Export's Lower Broadway headquarters during those years. "Genoa heard of a huge, postwar migration of Europeans that was forming in Italy, Spain and even southern Germany. With the Italian Line still paralyzed from wartime losses, Export management saw this flow of low-fare traffic - migrants as well as refugees, dependents, even displaced persons - as a viable business... And so, we chartered five transports [the 12,500 ton, 900 passenger *Marine Shark, Marine Carp, Marine Flasher, Marine Perch,* and *Marine Jumper*] from the Government, from the Maritime Administration."

"They were very basic, very simple ships. They offered very little to passengers other than transport. They sailed mostly to Italian ports, to Naples and Genoa. Later, in 1949, we experimented with an extended service to Haifa. We carried many, many immigrants ... and many of them were landed in Canada, during a westbound call at Halifax, or were sent by train to Toronto after landing at New York.".

American Export next tried a series of conversions of wartime troop transport ships. "By 1947-48, however, American

Queen Mary Ferrying Troops to Europe, 1942

LaGuardia, In Dock, With Constitution Behind

Export wanted
to upgrade its status in the passen-
ger ship business," remembers Herb Maletz. "The char-
ters for those Marine Class ships were dropped gradually and a succession
of far more comfortable passenger ships was added..." The first experiment
was the conversion of four transports as the new "Four Aces" [the 9,600
ton *Excalibur, Excambion, Exeter,* and *Exochorda*] which were combined
passenger/cargo ships. They sailed on continuous 44-day itineraries, from
New York to Marseilles, Naples, Alexandria, Jaffa, Tel Aviv, Haifa, Beirut,
Piraeus, Leghorn, Genoa, Marseilles and then homeward to New York via

Boston. "They were fantastic ships on the inside," said Herb Maletz. "They had great style, intimacy like big, luxury yachts; they were pure first class, only 125 berths in all. James Cagney took all the berths on one sailing and invited friends for the entire 44-day trip. These ships were very popular and were always wait listed. Their superb style and accommodations were in fact 'test runs' for the larger *Independence* and *Constitution*."

American Export's last experiment in troopship conversion was the *General W. P. Richardson,* a 622-foot long ship built to carry 5,200 troops with 144,000 cubic feet of military cargo. (The government had hoped to rebuild all eleven ships of this type to commercial, passenger-carrying service.) She was rebuilt to moderate rather than luxurious accommodations for 609 passengers, 157 in first class and 452 in tourist, and renamed *LaGuardia* in honor of the City's beloved mayor, the late Fiorello H. LaGuardia. At first, she sailed only to Italy, to Naples and Genoa; later itineraries expanded to include Gibraltar, Palermo, Piraeus and Haifa. Herb Maletz recalls, "The *LaGuardia,* even as a prelude and a 'test case' for the *Independence* and *Constitution*, was a failure. She was a loser from day one. She had operational problems. She was too expensive. And she had very high crew wages, including some who had 40-45 hours a week of just overtime!". Her original design had been to military specifications. She had double engine rooms and extra hull plating, which caused extra drag. Her fuel costs were beyond even the wildest estimates. Even though the *La Guardia* sailed with capacity loads in each direction, including a fair share of westbound Italian immigrants, American

Exeter, One of the Post-War "Four Aces"

*American Export
Annual Report, 1949*

Export quickly canceled charter arrangements with the Government. (Other lines watched the problems of the *Richardson* and rapidly dropped plans for conversions to passenger carriers).

All of these conversions of wartime troop ships had not produced the great ships which the government (even in its scaled back program) wanted and American Export was eager to produce. Herb Maletz recalls, "From the very start, in 1947-48, the two new American Export luxury liners were conceived as great ships with top class accommodations, especially in first class. John Slater, the financial genius who was then the president of American Export Lines, wanted big liners like the United States Lines. He was jealous of that company and very much admired their beautiful *America*. When word spread that United States Lines was planning an Atlantic supership [the *United States*], Slater insisted on big liners for Export's Mediterranean service. But he also insisted that these new, three-class liners must also be like cruise ships, large versions of our post-war 'Four Aces' with their club-like 125 berths." For all of Slater's enthusiasm, it is important to remember that it was the atmosphere of the Cold War, the fear of World War III, and the potential of conversion of liners to troopships which triggered their construction. Only this atmosphere made it politically possible to get government subsidies from Congress. Without them, no ships would have been built.

American Export's Annual Report for 1947 revealed that, "Plans for two new liners are now in the hands of the Technical Division of the United States Maritime Commission and are being sent to shipbuilders for bids. Toward the middle of the year we will know what aid we may expect from the Government, what total cost will amount to, and whether or not we will proceed with the construction under a Construction Subsidy."

A year later, American Export's Annual Report stated, "A most important step was taken by your Company during the year 1948 in the agreement which was reached between the United States Maritime Commission for the construction of two large passenger liners." Bids were requested on April 1,

1948 and opened on June 2. Building the mighty *Independence* and *Constitution* were two of the most prized maritime construction projects of the immediate postwar era. "It was the most sought-after shipbuilding contract in America at the time. It was second only to the building of the larger *United States*," said Frank Braynard who was a maritime reporter in New York at that time. Newport News Shipbuilding & Dry Dock Company in Virginia was interested, as was the New York Shipbuilding Corporation of Camden, New Jersey. It was the Bethlehem Steel Company, however, which landed the $50,000,000 order for the American Export twins of which the government would pay approximately half under the terms of the Merchant Marine Act of 1936. In the 1930's, Bethlehem's Quincy, Massachusetts yard had had considerable experience building passenger ships. They created a trio of stylish luxury vessels for the Matson Line's Hawaii and South Pacific service, and three ships for the Panama Railroad Company's Caribbean service.

In all, ten vessels were under contract to Quincy in 1949; these represented orders worth $150,000,000. To the city of Quincy and its surroundings, these ships offered profitable work for 9,500 persons, the largest peacetime force of the yard's 50 year history. Alone, the *Independence* and *Constitution* represented the largest passenger ship order ever placed in New England.

Very Early Rendering of the Constitution

CHAPTER THREE:
CONSTRUCTION, CELEBRATION,
AND FIRST VOYAGE

Shipbuilders at the Quincy yard laid the first keel plate for the *Independence* on March 29, 1949; work on the *Constitution* began only four months later. In July, the *New York Times* reported, "The *Independence* and the *Constitution* are designed to accommodate 1,000 passengers each in what would be the best equipment aboard any American craft, symbolizing like their name, 'the very finest in American culture'. The ships will be the first fully air-conditioned big liners ever to be built and will incorporate all the latest improvements in streamlining, design, construction and equipment. Both are expected to be ready for service late next year. The complete order for steel already is in storage at the yard. Since they are being built under the Merchant Marine Act of 1936, with a construction differential and additional allowances for national defense requirements, the ships readily may be converted into troopships with a capacity of 5,000 men. Following the brief keel-laying ceremony [for the *Constitution*], officials went to one of the yard warehouses where a complete first class stateroom had been assembled for inspection. Features of the equipment are two Pullman wall berths and a sofa berth to accommodate three passengers, with a maximum of living space and adjoining bath. In addition to the air conditioning, the stateroom also has an adjustable, polaroid porthole."

Moving A Section Of The Hull Structure

An article in the *New York Times* dated February 24, 1950 announced that construction of these two Export liners was well underway. "Officials of American Export Lines said yesterday that the *Independence* was about 32% completed on February 1st and the *Constitution* about 25%. Design changes, however, have set back the delivery dates to January and April 1951 respectively."

The Great Propellers of the Independence

American Export and Bethlehem Steel released details of two further distinctions of these new liners. First, they required the largest bull gears (main propeller shaft driving gears) ever produced in the United States. Each bull gear weighed 45 tons and measured over 17 feet in diameter. They were produced by the Falk Gear Corporation of Milwaukee. Second, the bow assemblies for each ship were among the largest ever prefabricated for an American merchant vessel. When the bow for each ship was assembled at Quincy, each weighed 142 tons and had a height of 54 feet. They were so large that Bethlehem engineers had to cut them into fore and aft sections to fit them into place. Twelve thousand tons of steel went into each liner

Propellers Crossing the George Washington Bridge

31

(roughly equivalent to 8000 1950 Fords); each ship also required 315,000 pounds of welding rod, such as the engine and boiler foundations. For safety, the liners had separate engine rooms capable of operating as independent units. Each was equipped with four 1,100—kilowatt generators (comparable capacity to a city of 20,000). An auxiliary generator was installed on the Sun Deck for emergency use. The navigational equipment included two types of radar and the Sperry gyrocompass. The safety features included 14 watertight transverse bulkheads, Johns Manville fireproofing material in the interiors and Walter Kidde fire fighting equipment.

Henry Dreyfuss Considering a Design Problem

For the interior of the ships, American Export turned to the famous industrial designer Henry Dreyfuss, then at the peak of a long and distinguished career. Among thousands of projects, he and his firm had designed the Twentieth Century Limited train, the Hoover vacuum cleaner, the rotary telephone, the circular Honeywell thermostat, and most of the John Deere tractors. Dreyfus saw no conflict between the arts and mass production. "It is my contention that well-designed, mass-produced goods constitute a new American art form and are responsible for the creation of a new American culture. These products of the applied arts are a part of everyday American living and working, not merely museum pieces to be seen on a Sunday afternoon."

It was this commitment to functional design and ease of use which generated the designer's "yardstick" for any design problem. A well-designed object should have high utility and safety, low maintenance, a reasonable first cost, good sales appeal, and pleasing overall appearance. Throughout the 1930's and 40's Dreyfuss was one of the passionate advocates of the science we now call ergonomics. His firm measured humans by the thousands - standing, sitting, walking, bending - in support of the then-radical idea that the best lever, handle, color, or layout could enhance safety and comfort in any job or situation. The items of everyday use on the ship were, then, to have a consciously "American" feel, and conform to Dreyfuss' standards of good design. As he put it a few years later, in *Designing For People:*

"The interior of an ocean liner constitutes what is perhaps the most complex problem that can be presented to an industrial designer. Inherent in the problem is the fact that a great ship becomes for a number of days the home of a thousand or more men, women, and children who are completely dependent on the ship for their safety, comfort, and well-being. The designer must keep all of this in mind as he lays out the staterooms and public rooms; as he selects colors, fabrics, chinaware, cutlery, floor coverings, leather, wall decorations, key-identification tabs, lighting fixtures, draperies, soundproofing, air conditioning, drawer pulls, beds, chairs, rubber tile for dance floors - and the thousands of other elements involved."

Pre-Launch Rendering of Aft Lounge

Rendering of Boat 'n' Bottle Bar

Pre-Launch Rendering of Stateroom by Day

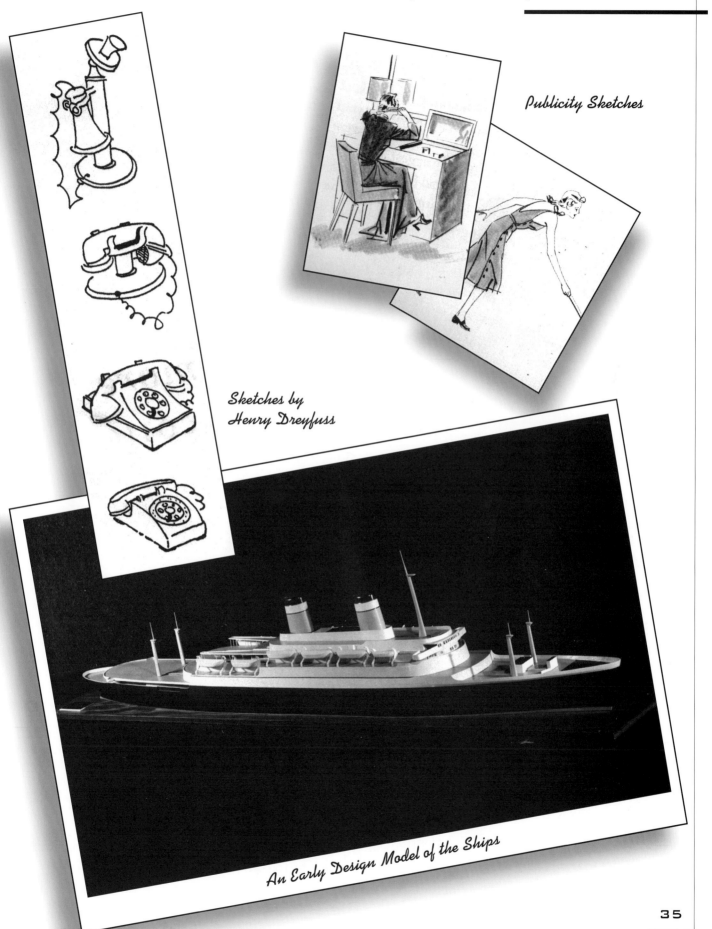

Publicity Sketches

Sketches by Henry Dreyfuss

An Early Design Model of the Ships

Pre-Launch Rendering of Aft Decks

Many of these "design" solutions were much more than just form as Dreyfuss further recalled in *Designing For People:*

"Before World War II, stewards remained on duty twenty-four hours a day, with only cat naps, and rested at the end of the voyage. Under a revision of the working conditions, they went on eight-hour shifts. This meant that, if Export Line was to continue full-time personal service, three times as many stewards would have to be fed, provided with sleeping quarters, and cared for in foreign ports, a considerable added expense. The solution was found by revising the housekeeping system for passenger quarters. Passenger-operated beds, which slipped into position for sleeping when a foot pedal was pressed, were installed. Through such innovations, a full complement of stewards on night duty became unnecessary and the line was able to provide better maintenance and service with fewer people."

Overall, American Export liked what it saw from the Henry Dreyfuss' design firm. In the spring of 1950, just months from the launching of the *Independence*, the company issued a press release filled with pride in the interiors.

Pre-Launch Rendering of Stateroom by Night

"Dreyfuss, charged to provide the utmost comfort for every passenger in each of the three classes as well as American living standards for the 575 officers and crew, has produced innumerable refinements that set new standards for living at sea. Spacious, bright color combinations, exclusive fabric designs and weaves for drapery and upholstery, private baths, ample dresser, wardrobe and baggage storage space and air conditioning are stateroom features. Oversized folding wall and sofa berths permit instant conversion of bedrooms into spacious living rooms."

"The atmosphere of a fine American home is evidenced further in the magnificent series of public rooms that occupy the entire Promenade Deck," the releases continued.

"Forward is a circular Observation Lounge 65 feet in diameter with broad windows looking out to sea for two thirds of its circumference. Aft is the library with a special niche to enshrine a copy of the 'Declaration of Independence,' and with an interesting furniture arrangement to provide conversational privacy for small groups. Still farther aft are the Cocktail Lounges for first and cabin class passengers. Surrounding the sweep of rooms is a broad Promenade Deck. There are 8 large suites, two of which have private enclosed verandahs. A large theatre, sunken-floor dining room, gymnasium, electric baths, shops, elevators and intra-ship as well as ship-to-shore telephones are among the additional attractions."

"There are large swimming pools for first and cabin class passengers and a salt water cascade for tourists. The first class pool of Hollywood design, tapered, with rounded corners and underwater illumination for nighttime use, is the center of interest of the two level Sun Club sports area that altogether covers over 9,000 square feet. The deck above the vast pool area extends aft in two broad wings to multiply the lounging area for spectators who wish to view the swimming. Forward of the pool is the Sun Club Cafe, which includes an American soda bar. Large sections of the glass after-wall and roof of this room can be rolled back to convert it into an open-air terrace."

Mrs. Slater Christens the Independence

John E. Slater, the President of American Export, added at the time, "The *Independence* and her sistership, the *Constitution*, which will soon follow, represent an all-out bid to win and hold trans-Atlantic travelers by providing American flag ships tailored to the American standard of living."

The *Independence* was launched on Saturday, June 3rd, a warm, spring day at Quincy. Weeks before, scaffolding on the hull was removed. The fresh paint of the hull gleamed. As the ship slid down the ways into the Weymouth River, the launch process directly involved 650 people, all under the direction of Bethlehem Steel managers and engineers. Some 110 were onboard the ship itself while the other 440 were ashore. To smooth the slipway passage, 25,845 pounds of hard grease and over 20,000 pounds of slip grease were applied to the ways. A Bethlehem official said, "Long before any of the notables of the launching party are in their seats on the reviewing stand, the actual work of loosening the grip of the *Independence* will begin. At one minute after midnight on June 3rd, grease irons will be removed, followed by some shoring at 2:30 and 3 A.M. Then, gradually as the hour of launching approaches, more and more wedges and then keelblocks, all in carefully planned sequence, are knocked out. In the last hour before the event at 2 P.M., preparations reach an accelerated tempo as the final bilge cribs are slipped out, final trigger tests held, and the gangway and temporary light and fire alarm connections removed. Launching the *Independence* at 2 P.M. is scheduled to take maximum advantage of the high tide, which will reach a height of 9.5 feet at close to that hour."

Over 10,000 people attended the launch ceremonies. A large contingent of representatives of the US Government travelled from Washington for the ceremonies in a 19-car special train, which picked up another substantial group including press representatives at New York. It was the biggest crowd in US history ever to view a launching.

Going Down the Ways

D. D. Strohmeier, Vice President of Bethlehem Steel, acted as the master of ceremonies. Mrs. John E. Slater, wife of the American Export Lines' President, cracked the traditional bottle of champagne over the bow at precisely 2 o'clock. Immediately afterward, the big hull went down the ways. The launching turned Quincy into a holiday town, jamming its highways and railroads. Townspeople, many of them from the families of the shipyard's employees, began to pour through the Bethlehem Steel gates at noon. A large delegation came from nearby Boston.

But amidst the cheer, the excitement, and the rousing, congratulatory speeches, Bethlehem's Vice President Strohmeier spoke in a different vein. He said, "The launching of the *Independence* turned another slipway into idleness and was another step in the crippling paralysis that is gripping American shipyards. Not one keel for a sea going vessel remains to be laid in the United States. Yet we have only one-third of the passenger ships we had pre-war and less than half the pre-war troop lift capacity. Three years ago, the President's Advisory Committee on the Merchant Marine stated that an efficient fleet and a progressive shipbuilding industry were indispensable to the national security.

Lowering a Funnel Into Place

Reviewing the dearth of passenger and potential troop transport tonnage, the Committee recommended a minimum of 46 passenger ships to be built by 1951. What happened to this program? Because of public and governmental apathy, our erstwhile shipbuilding potential could easily result in the loss of World War III. There is work to be done. It is time to wake up!"

Following the *Independence* and then the *Constitution*, American Export would never again build new passenger liners. America itself would create only four more luxury ships, two for the Grace Line and a pair for the Moore-McCormack Lines, all of them in 1958. Quincy would never again build liners and, except for a quartet of passenger-container combination ships for the Grace Line, Bethlehem Steel would never again have passenger ships to their credit. While there were plans for other American passenger ships, such as the projected 43,000-ton President Washington for American President Lines' trans-Pacific service, they never left the drawing boards. Money, particularly those much-needed subsidies from Washington, was the key obstacle.

Henry Dreyfuss' interior design came together rapidly in the closing months of 1950. In October, writing for the *New York Herald Tribune*, shipping editor Walter Hamshar made a tour of the *Independence* at Quincy and did a comprehensive review of the ship's progress. "From the exterior, the big ship appears almost ready for service," he noted. "Inside the big liner, the first to be constructed in this country in a decade, the guess on completion date

Assembling the Deck

Caulking the Deck

would depend on which part of the ship is inspected. Many rooms on the lower decks are ready to be lived in now, while on the upper decks only the outlines of the future luxurious lounges and suites are visible. The Bethlehem yard has 2,600 workers on the ship and another 1,000 in shops rushing to complete the liner. Yard officials are confident the *Independence* will be ready for her builder's trials on December 5th to 8th; her delivery run from Boston to New York will be in early January and her first sailing, a 53-day cruise to the Mediterranean, on February 8th."

Hamshar continued, "The outside appearance of the new liner is inspiring. Since she was launched last June 3rd, the *Independence* has assumed a permanent form. The mast, two funnels and kingposts have been stepped and painted; her lifeboats have been slung; and her rounded bridge structure freed from scaffolding. Workmen are putting the final touches to her weather decks, laying two-and-a-half inch spruce planking and then caulking the seams. The last pieces of mosaic tile on the first class pool on the Sun Deck were laid last week. The pool for the cabin and tourist passengers on the Main Deck also is ready for service. It is a portable pool fitting over the hatch cover to the liner's No. 6 cargo hold."

"Interior accommodations are furthest along on C Deck, the lowest deck with living quarters. At least half the tourist and crew rooms there are completed and painters are putting the finishing touches on many of the remaining rooms. As these rooms are readied for service, they are locked, pending the day the *Independence* will set out for waters off Maine for her sea trials. A tour of the tourist class and crew quarters show them to be among the most pleasant and comfortable afloat. Only two passenger rooms will have as many as six berths; all crew rooms are limited to no more than four seamen. Crew members and passengers alike will control the temperature and humidity in their rooms by a turn of the air-conditioning dials. The ship's theater, located on C Deck, is the first public room near completion. The carpet was laid in this room last week and installation of seats for 154 persons will ready it for service. The theater will be used interchangeably as a chapel by using a portable altar."

"Work on the two engines that will drive the Independence at a 25-knot top speed has reached the testing stage," he noted. "The boilers have been manufacturing steam for several weeks. This week's schedule [October 22nd] calls for the liner's generators to be turned on so that the liner will begin furnishing some of the power to be used in the interior construction. The two giant propellers were fitted to their 24-inch shafts before the launching."

"Completion of the *Independence* on schedule has become the special project of every Quincy shipyard worker from John T. Wiseman,

Installation Of One Of The Ship's Boilers

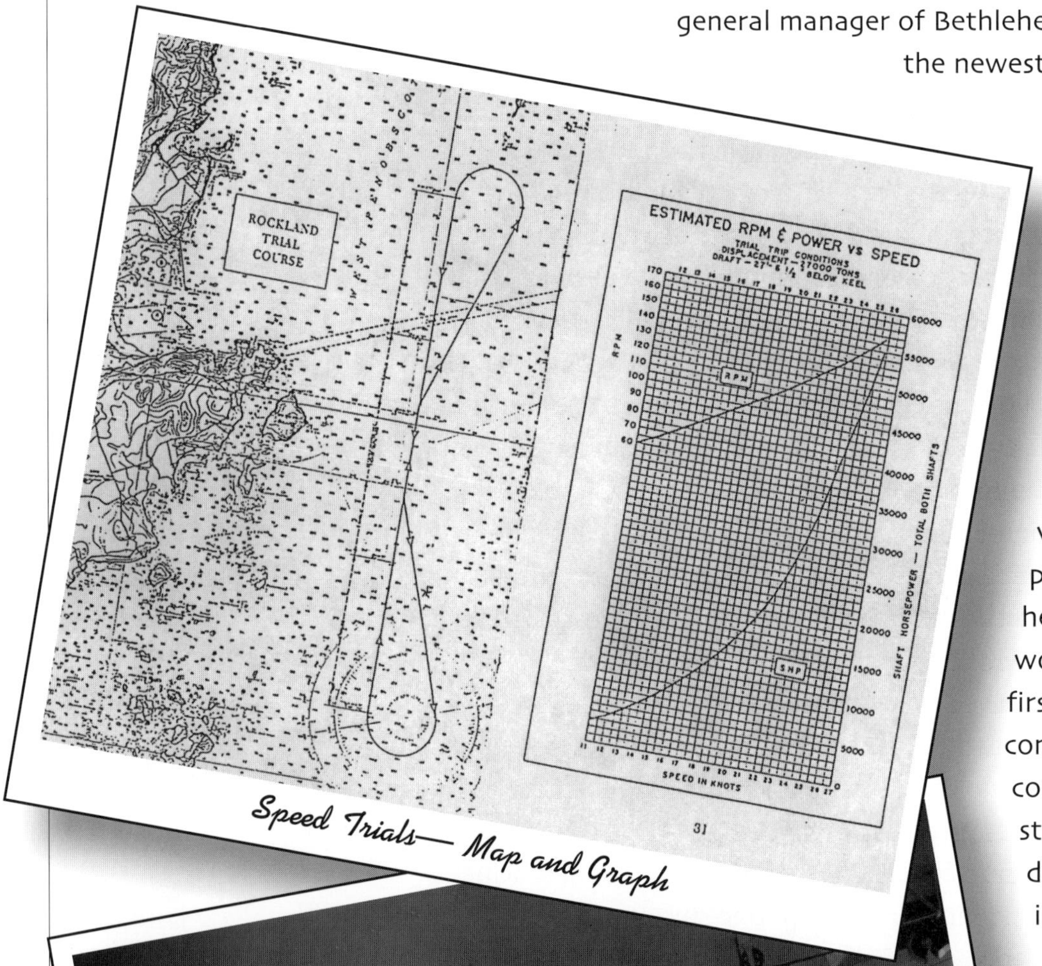

Speed Trials— Map and Graph

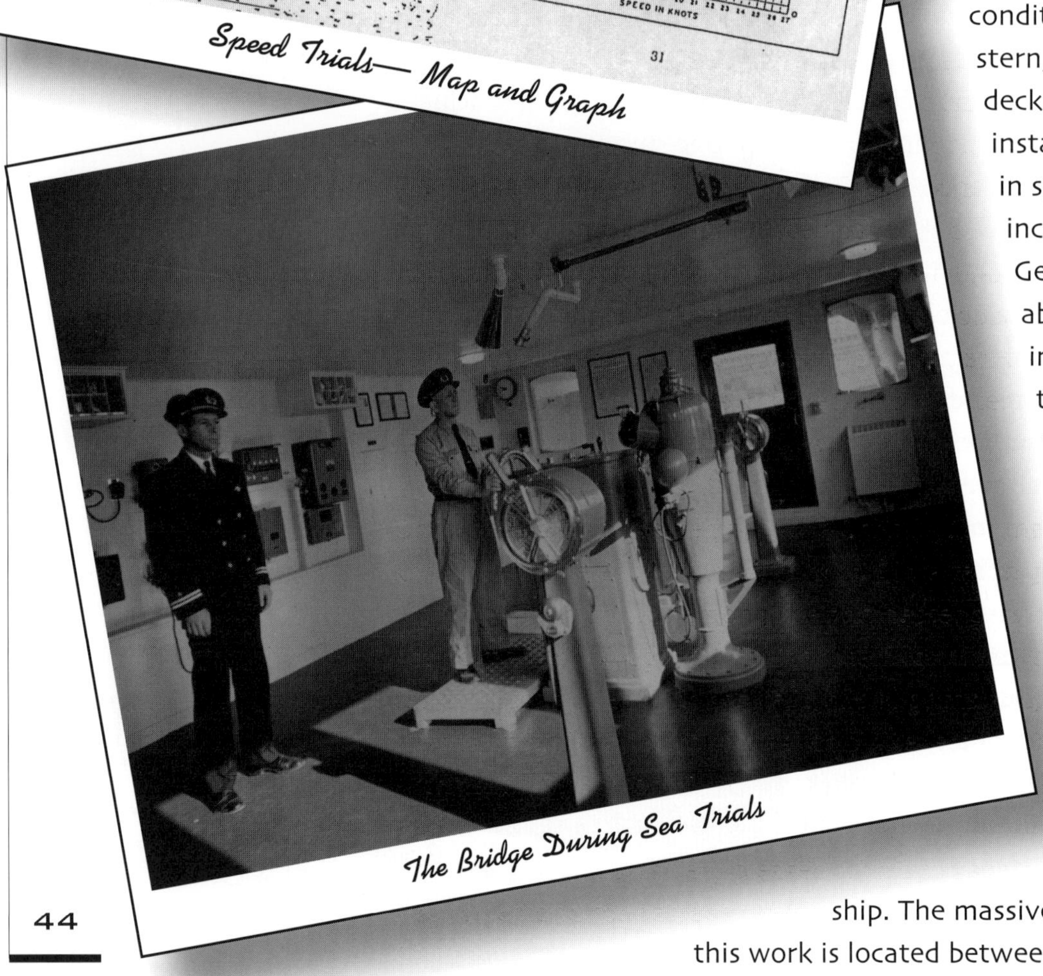

The Bridge During Sea Trials

general manager of Bethlehem Steel's Boston district, to the newest helper of skilled craftsmen at work in every part of the ship," concluded Hamshar. "It is nearest to the heart of Herbert Chubbuck, way foreman, who has had supervision of the big vessel since her keel was laid. Mr. Chubbuck knows the location of virtually every nut and bolt in the vessel. But the *Independence* posed a special problem for her construction engineers and workers because she will be the first big passenger liner ever constructed equipped with air conditioning from stem to stern, and from keel to bridge deck. This has required the installation of miles of ducts in spaces where every cubic inch is at a premium. Generally the ducts run above the passageway ceilings, side by side with electric power-line ducts and water mains. Above the ceiling of one passageway, workmen fitted 29 different types of ducts and pipes. Seventeen fan rooms will drive heated or cooled air to every part of the ship after it is sucked in through vents on the top of the ship. The massive machinery that will do this work is located between the two engine rooms.

The conditioning units are geared to change all the air of every stateroom every seven minutes and every public room every twelve minutes."

In the fall of 1950, American Export began sales for the 53-day maiden voyage, a gala Mediterranean cruise. The trip would call at 22 ports in 13 countries, including Tangier, Haifa, Beirut, Alexandria, Istanbul and Naples. Minimum fare was $1,500 per person for an inside room with two lower berths on C Deck, shared toilet and shower (This would be about $18,000 in today's prices). The two penthouses on the Sun Deck, consisting of a bedroom, living room, two private bathrooms, twin dressing rooms, twin baggage areas and a private verandah, cost $10,000 per person. The Suites De Luxe, consisting of two bedrooms, a living room, three bathrooms and three baggage areas, were slightly more expensive at $10,700 per person. A complete program of shore excursions and extended tours included, for example, a 4-day overland tour from Alexandria to Cairo, Luxor and Karnak priced at $337 per person. The inaugural cruise sold out quickly and passenger demand exceeded the company's greatest expectations.

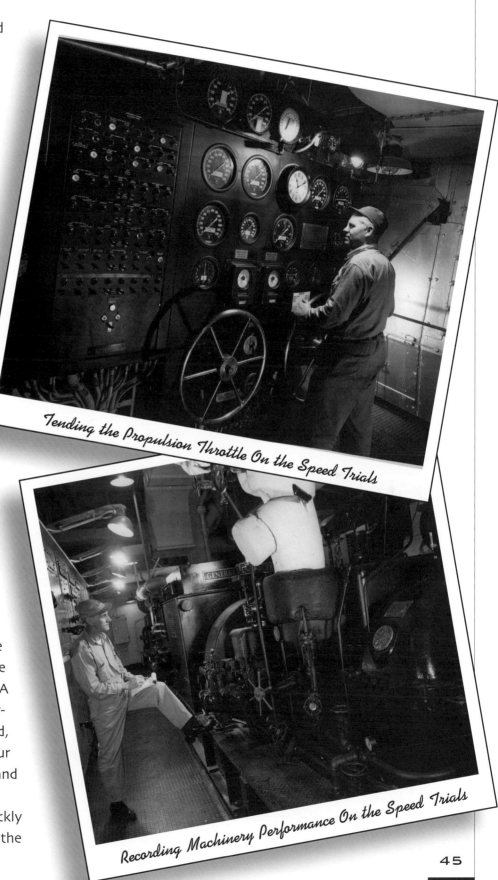

Tending the Propulsion Throttle On the Speed Trials

Recording Machinery Performance On the Speed Trials

The *Independence* left the Quincy yard on December 1st on the first sea trials: an overnight trip to test the two engine rooms, the air conditioning system, the wind resistance, and other technical features. She anchored for the night off Provincetown, returned to the Boston Naval Yard Annex in South Boston on Saturday morning, and was dry-docked in final preparation for more extensive sea trials the following week.

The speed trials were a blazing success. On Thursday, December 7th, she became the "Speed Queen of the American Merchant Marine." That afternoon, she steamed at a rate of 26.1 knots, surpassing by a full knot the previous record held by United States Lines' *America*. The *Independence* conducted speed trials off the Maine coast and spent the night anchored off Rockland. On Friday morning, the ship returned to Boston and on Saturday morning arrived at nearby Quincy for final outfitting and adjustments and finishing touches to her first class quarters.

An Early Publicity Photo Session

The liner remained at Quincy over the Christmas-New Year holidays of 1950 and American Export took the opportunity to announce that the liner would have a "Fifth Avenue of Fine Shops" aboard. Saks Fifth Avenue would supply and staff a specialty shop, Brentano's the book shop and Helena Rubinstein the beauty salon. "This is the first time Saks Fifth Avenue has ever tried to operate a shop at sea," said Adam Gimbel, the department store president. "At Genoa, the *Independence* will take on fine European items as well including sweaters from Scotland, woolens from England, handbags from France, neckwear from Italy and clocks and watches from Switzerland."

Nothing interrupted the excitement, the anticipation, the hectic pace at American Export's Manhattan headquarters. The brand new *Independence* would arrive in a matter of weeks, in the third week of January. The first event in the inaugural schedule was a gala overnight "delivery" sailing from Boston to New York on Sunday, January 21st. The *Independence* left the Quincy yard on Friday morning, the 19th, and moved to the Commonwealth Pier in Boston harbor. Officials, company friends, the members of the press, and other guests boarded the liner on Saturday evening. On Sunday, the 20th, she departed at just after 6 AM with her 337 passengers. The course lay outside Cape Cod to the Nantucket Lightship, down the south shore of Long Island to Ambrose Lightship, and into New York harbor. Monday, January 21st, was a cold, clear day in New York. The *Independence* arrived at 10:30 AM at Pier 84, at the foot of West 44th Street. New York harbor was a lively scene that day. Six other passenger ships also docked - the *Brazil* (Moore McCormack Lines), the *Fort Amherst* (Furness Withy), the *Veragua* (United Fruit Company) the *Santa Barbara* (Grace Line), the *General H. Taylor* (International Refugee Organization), and the *Edam* (Holland America Line).

Another Publicity Photo Session

Frank Braynard, then a staff maritime reporter for the *New York Herald Tribune,* was aboard and recalls, "These overnight trips were organized by Max Brown, the public relations man for Bethlehem Steel. They were exquisite vessels in every way. They were big, beautiful, luxurious, powerful; in all, the perfect showcases for American technology and shipbuilding.

Many of us were especially fascinated by the counter sterns used on the ships. American Export preferred them for Italian dockings, at Genoa and at Naples, where ships tended to berth stern first. Export could use smaller piers because of the overhang of the stern ...They were fantastic symbols, wonderful vessels in every way ... The Boat'n Bottle Bar was exceptional and those two, winged decks around the first class pool was another highlight. Italian Line was not yet resurrected and so these Export liners were unquestionably the finest passenger liners sailing to and from the Med."

Another Publicity Photo

Also on the Boston-New York trip, *Herald Tribune* reporter Marion Conger paid tribute to the brilliance of Henry Dreyfuss' design work.

"...the most outstanding feature of the *Independence* is that she is so completely American, not only in the emphasis on safe, efficient mechanical operation, but in the planning and decor of all her rooms. Still, there is no hint of phony Colonial or garish ultra-modernistic decorative schemes that sometimes pass as typically American. Both public and private rooms have been designed and furnished to create a feeling of uncluttered spaciousness. Even the corridors, indirectly lighted and painted in soft gray green, lemon yellow or coral, provide vistas of color as one walks along them. Chairs upholstered in the finest leathers in chocolate browns or warm pastels are as comfortable as they are handsome. Drapes of heavy linen and other specially woven fabrics are rich in texture, but subdued in color, blending restfully with the wall areas when drawn."

"Even the smallest accessories, such as sugar wrappings and match folders, were designed with care by Henry Dreyfuss and his associates. Each of the three restaurants has its own china, napery, glass and silverware designed as an integral part of its decorative scheme. The artworks include an enormous revolving globe in one foyer and a magnetic map in another on which the ship's position can be plotted. Passengers were equally fascinated by the beautiful and exact scale model of the original frigate *Independence*, which is on display in a glass case. The recreational facilities include a new type of lightweight aluminum deck chair with colorful plastic webbing. One of the ship's finest public areas is the Sea Island Club, for first class passengers, an entirely new type of floating play area. Roll-away glass doors join the pool, done in colored glass mosaics, with the pool cafe and its glistening soda fountain. No two of the roomy staterooms, regardless of class, have been decorated alike. All first and cabin class rooms are equipped with telephones that have a 5000-mile range. Even tourist class rooms, some of which can accommodate six persons, are in no way cramped. Newly designed upper and lower bunks leave generous provisions for wardrobe and dresser space."

During her inaugural visit to New York, the *Independence* was open to the public on several afternoons from 2:30 until 5:30 PM. Over 10,000 people went aboard and contributed one dollar each to the Seamen's Welfare Committee. In total, 13,000 visitors inspected the *Independence* between her arrival on January 22nd and her departure February 10th on her maiden voyage. A highlight of the various receptions, luncheons and dinners held aboard was a supper dance attended by 1000 guests for the benefit of the Metropolitan Opera.

Late in January, the liner left port for a 3-day "preview cruise". Some 500 guests included Mayor Impellitteri of New York City, members of Congress, executives from other shipping companies, and members of the Maritime Commission and the Coast Guard. The liner sailed within a few miles of Bermuda and then turned back, exceeding her own record with a top speed of 26.8 knots for several brief periods.

Cover of the Maiden Voyage Brochure

Coffee Service by Henry Dreyfuss

Frank McCormack,
Superintendent Engineer at American Export,
later said, "The vessel's engines, while not quite at maximum revolutions developed the new speed level with a minimum vibration. The tests at sea included figure-eight runs for a study of stability. Fairly high winds and swells gave the engineers an opportunity to study performance in moderately rough seas." L.S. Andrews, Vice President in Charge of Operations at Export, added, "We were particularly pleased during this voyage with the results of the fuel tests showing a low rate of consumption, and with the two water evaporators for making fresh water from the sea. It is the first American vessel with complete water-making equipment. Using only one evaporator, the equipment developed water for drinking and other uses at the rate of 410 tons in 24 hours. A remarkable feature was that fresh water could be made at less than the cost of water at New York piers."

Just days before the first transatlantic sailing, there were troubles with the National Maritime Union, which filed a complaint that the manning scale aboard the liner was below contract specifications. In hasty meetings with the union, American Export officials agreed to add three additional quartermasters and more stewards. The union agreed to these changes, and released the ship to sail.

On Saturday, February 10th, the *Independence* left her berth at Pier 84 with 450 passengers and 578 crew members. Simultaneously, the liner *America* sailed from the adjacent berth at Pier 86, as did Holland America's *Noordam* from a berth across the Hudson in Hoboken, New Jersey. Other passenger ship departures from New York that same day included the *Queen Of Bermuda*, the *De Grasse*, the *Italia* and the *Rio Jachal*, each bound south, on cruises to Bermuda, the Caribbean and along the East Coast of South America.

Henry Dreyfuss Ashtray and Passenger Welcome

The *Independence* was enthusiastically received as she made her way around the Mediterranean in the late winter and early spring of 1951. She was a "gleaming symbol of Yankee ingenuity," as Fred Slater called her, to still-devastated Europe. By the time the liner called at Beirut, on March 3rd, the United States Information Service had assembled, printed, and issued a 26-page booklet of photos and press coverage of the *Independence* in the various ports she had visited.

Istanbul gave the liner a tremendous welcome on March 16th. (Ironically, the national flagship, the 9,900 ton *Tarsus*, was in port as well. She had been the *Exochorda* of 1931, one of American Export's original "Four Aces".) American Export's New York office reported, "Istanbul roared with a tremendous welcome for the *Independence*. It even challenged New York for leadership and excitement. Hundreds of craft, including other liners, ferries, tugs and yachts, jammed the Golden Horn docks and anchorages on both sides of the Bosphorous and tied-down their whistles. And hundreds of

TWO ON DECK

"... I WAS AMONG SEVERAL HUNDRED GUESTS
INVITED TO GO BY SPECIAL TRAIN
FROM NEW YORK TO BOSTON
THE DAY THE INDEPENDENCE WAS TO
SAIL FROM THE QUINCY SHIPYARDS,
AND RIDE BACK FOR THE GALA RECEPTION
NEW YORK HARBOR GIVES NEW LINERS.
AT THE LAST MOMENT I CANCELLED
MY TRAIN RESERVATION AND TOOK A PLANE.
I WANTED TO WALK ON THE FINISHED SHIP ALONE,
BEFORE THE HUNDREDS OF WELL WISHERS ARRIVED.
WHEN I WALKED UP THE GANGPLANK,
THE GREAT SHIP SEEMED ALMOST DESERTED.
BUT AS I APPROACHED THE LENGTH OF ITS DECK,
I SAW A SOLITARY FIGURE APPROACHING
AND I RECOGNIZED JOHN SLATER.
HE, TOO, FELT THE URGE TO BE ALONE
WITH HIS COMPLETED DREAM.
WE WALKED THE SHIP TOGETHER ...
AS WE COMPLETED THE INSPECTION,
HE SAID, 'I WOULDN'T CHANGE A SINGLE THING'. "

HENRY DREYFUSS,
"DESIGNING FOR PEOPLE"

*Henry Dreyfuss' Sketch
of Two On Deck*

thousands of spectators on both the European and Asiatic shores crowded all windows and rooftops. Friendly inhabitants waved flags, bed-sheets, handkerchiefs and everything else available. Auto and truck horns violating the local law on silence joined in the chorus. Later, government Customs and Immigration threw away the rule books to make things simple and convenient for the passengers aboard the sparkling new liner. The *Independence* continued 17 miles through the Bosphorous to enable passengers to look at the Black Sea. Later, while anchored off Domabatche, a special program of Turkish folk music and dancing was arranged by the Turkish Government. The American Ambassador invited American Export officials and officers to cocktails at the American Legation. Radio Ankara made tape recordings of passenger impressions of their visit to Istanbul for later broadcast to English-speaking countries outside the Turkish capital."

At Piraeus, the port for Athens, King Paul and Queen Frederika of Greece came aboard and stayed for four hours instead of the one hour protocol visit they had originally scheduled. A separate reception was held for members of the Greek shipping community, including representatives from the Goulandris, Livanos, Niarchos and Onassis companies.

Genoa was another port that gave special honors to the new liner. Passengers were invited to a reception at the historic Palazzo San Giorgio under the auspices of the Ente Provinciale per II Turismo, the government tourist agency for Genoa and the Italian Riviera. Other selected passengers were entertained by the Propeller Club of Genoa at a reception at the Hotel Savoia Majestic. Onboard the ship an evening program of elaborate Italian songs and dances was presented with music by the Ligurian Chorus.

Entire Crew on Aft Decks (Life Magazine Cover Photo Series)

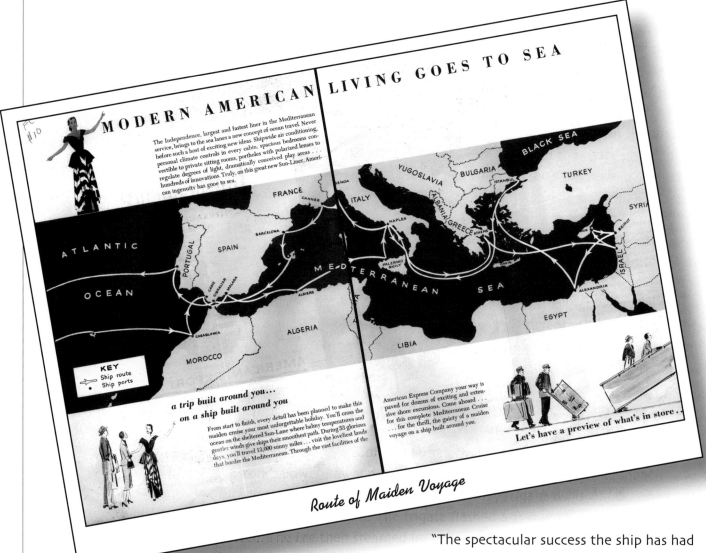

MODERN AMERICAN LIVING GOES TO SEA

The Independence, largest and fastest liner in the Mediterranean service, brings to the sea lanes a new concept of ocean travel. Never before such a host of exciting new ideas. Shipwide air conditioning, personal climate controls in every cabin, spacious bedrooms convertible to private sitting rooms, portholes with polarized lenses to regulate degrees of light, dramatically conceived play areas . . . hundreds of innovations. Truly, on this great new Sun-Liner, American ingenuity has gone to sea.

KEY
→ Ship route
• Ship ports

*a trip built around you . . .
on a ship built around you*

From start to finish, every detail has been planned to make this maiden cruise your most unforgettable holiday. You'll cross the ocean on the sheltered Sun-Lane where balmy temperatures and gentler winds give ships their smoothest path. During 53 glorious days, you'll travel 13,000 sunny miles . . . visit the loveliest lands that border the Mediterranean. Through the vast facilities of the American Express Company your way is paved for dozens of exciting and extensive shore excursions. Come aboard . . . for this complete Mediterranean Cruise . . . for the thrill, the gaiety of a maiden voyage on a ship built around you.

Let's have a preview of what's in store . . .

Route of Maiden Voyage

"The spectacular success the ship has had in making a friendly conquest of the Mediterranean makes her, we believe, an outstanding Ambassador of Good Will and showpiece of the modern American Way of Life," noted John Slater, the American Export President, who was aboard for the entire 53-day cruise.

At Cannes, the *Independence* remained at anchor for two days. All the yachts in the harbor were dressed in flags for the occasion and every passenger was presented with flowers upon landing. The Mayor of Cannes held a welcome champagne party for the ship and a cultural performance was held at the new Municipal Auditorium in the ship's honor.

The last week of the maiden voyage included a passenger auction of unwanted souvenirs, an April Fools' Day Masquerade Fancy Dress Ball and the Captain's Farewell Dinner. The passengers' final view of foreign soil was a memorable one. As the homebound *Independence* passed close to the

Azores, airplanes swooped near to the liner in bridge-height salutes. After 22 ports of call, the liner docked just after midday in New York City at Pier 84 on Wednesday, April 4th.

After the maiden voyage, American Export announced that the *Independence* had maintained an average speed of 23 knots during the 13,000 mile journey. "Her performance was consistently better than that shown on her sea trials," said one Company official. "Both in revolutions per minute as well as fuel consumption, she was amazing!" Eight days later, she departed on a special extended express voyage that included Piraeus, a port of convenience for four hundred Greeks from North America visiting their former homeland during "Home-Coming Year" celebrations. Later, following several months of regular transatlantic sailing, the *Independence* was dry-docked within New York harbor for the required bottom survey. She used the 700-foot long floating dock at Bethlehem Steel's yard at the foot of 56th Street in Brooklyn. Both the *Independence* and the *Constitution* would use this plant each year until 1964, when Bethlehem closed that yard and moved the large floating dock to its concentrated facilities at nearby Hoboken, New Jersey.

Construction on the *Constitution* shadowed her sister ship, starting on July 12, 1949. She was launched fourteen months later, September 16, 1950, with about 14,000 tons of steel erected. For the occasion, the Company's public relations department issued details similar to the christening staged for the *Independence* three months before.

ITINERARY MEDITERRANEAN CRUISE
Independence
EXCITING SHORE EXCURSIONS

53 DAYS
22 PORTS

Port	Arrive	Depart	Time in Port Days / Hours
New York		Sat. Feb. 10, Noon	10
Madeira	Fri. Feb. 16, 7:00 AM	Fri. Feb. 16, 5:00 PM	6
Casablanca (for Marrakesh, Rabat, Fez, and Meknes)	Sat. Feb. 17, 4:00 PM	Sun. Feb. 18, 10:00 PM	16½
Cadiz (for Seville, Granada, and the Alhambra)	Mon. Feb. 19, 7:30 AM	Mon. Feb. 19, Midnight	5
Gibraltar	Tue. Feb. 20, 7:00 AM	Tue. Feb. 20, Noon	12
Tangier	Tue. Feb. 20, 2:00 PM	Wed. Feb. 21, 2:00 AM	12
Malaga	Wed. Feb. 21, 7:00 AM	Wed. Feb. 21, 7:00 PM	23
Algiers (for the Kasbah)	Thu. Feb. 22, 1:00 PM	Fri. Feb. 23, Noon	10
Palermo (for Monreale)	Sat. Feb. 24, 1:00 PM	Sat. Feb. 24, 11:00 PM	16
Naples (for Pompeii, Amalfi, and Sorrento)	Sat. Feb. 25, 8:00 AM	Sun. Feb. 25, Midnight	16½
Athens (for the Parthenon and Acropolis)	Sun. Feb. 27, 8:30 AM	Wed. Feb. 28, 1:00 AM	2 / 17½
Haifa (for Israel: Tel-Aviv, The Holy Land, Nazareth, Tiberias, Capernaum, Jerusalem-in-Israel, Mt. Carmel)	Tue. Mar. 1, 7:30 AM	Sun. Mar. 4, 1:00 AM	15½
Larnaca (Cyprus)	Thu. Mar. 4, 8:30 AM	Sun. Mar. 4, Midnight	12
Beirut (for Damascus, Baalbeck, Jerusalem-in-Hashemite-Transjordan, Bethlehem, Mount of Olives)	Sun. Mar. 5, 7:00 AM	Wed. Mar. 7, 7:00 PM	2 / 12
Alexandria (for Cairo, the Pyramids, and Luxor)	Mon. Mar. 8, Noon	Tue. Mar. 13, 4:00 PM	5 / 4
Istanbul	Thu. Mar. 15, 2:00 PM	Sat. Mar. 17, 10:00 AM	1 / 20
Naples (for Capri, Rome, and Florence)	Mon. Mar. 19, 7:00 AM	Wed. Mar. 21, 9:00 PM	2 / 14
Genoa (for Rapallo, Santa Margherita, Portofino and the Italian Riviera)	Thu. Mar. 22, 2:00 PM	Sat. Mar. 24, 1:00 AM	1 / 11
Cannes (for Nice, Monte Carlo, Grasse, and the French Riviera)	Sat. Mar. 24, 7:00 AM	Mon. Mar. 26, 1:00 AM	1 / 18
Barcelona	Mon. Mar. 26, 1:00 PM	Mon. Mar. 26, Midnight	11
Palma (Capital of the Balearic Islands)	Mon. Mar. 27, 7:00 AM	Tue. Mar. 27, 6:00 PM	11
Gibraltar	Tue. Mar. 28, 2:00 PM	Wed. Mar. 28, 4:00 PM	2
Lisbon (for Cintra, Belem, Estoril and Fatima)	Wed. Mar. 29, 7:00 AM	Thu. Mar. 29, Midnight	17
New York	Wed. Apr. 4, 11:00 AM		

LITHO U. S. A. 10-50—25M

Maiden Voyage Itinerary

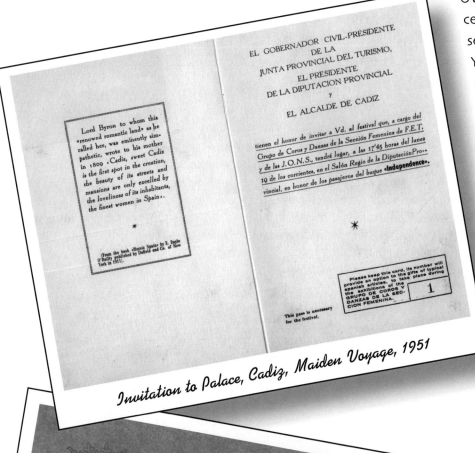

Invitation to Palace, Cadiz, Maiden Voyage, 1951

Pass to Palace, Cadiz, Maiden Voyage, February 1951

Over 15,000 people attended the ceremonies, some brought by a seventeen-car train from New York and Washington. 45,000 lbs. of grease were used to prepare the slipways. A bottle of California wine christened the hull because, as Export officials explained, "It is in keeping with the strictly American character of the new ship." At the launching, the liner's sponsor was Mrs. Charles Ulrick Bay, the wife of the American Ambassador to Norway. Mr. Bay was a director as well as important stockholder of American Export.

Less than a month later, the New York office announced that Captain Bernt A. Jacobsen, the master of the combo liner *Exeter*, would be the first captain of the *Constitution*. Work continued on the ship throughout the winter of 1950-51. Because of some material shortages caused by the Korean War, American Export delayed the April 24th maiden departure from New York to June 21st. The ship's trials were held on May 24-25th off the Massachusetts coast near Cape Cod. Actual delivery date to American Export was June 8th.

Rumors circulated that the *Constitution* would better the 26.1 knot record set by the *Independence* during her trials the previous December off the Maine coast. However, on May 25th, a release from Bethlehem Steel said, "There would be no attempt made today by the *Constitution* to break the 26.105 knot speed record set late last year by the *Independence*." There were actually two sets of tests, one on May 24th and the second on the 25th. During the night, the new liner anchored in the President's Roads in lower Boston harbor.

With trials completed, the *Constitution* left the Quincy yard on June 9th and moved to Boston's big Commonwealth Pier. On Sunday, June 10th, six New England governors along with five hundred civic, business, and religious leaders attended a reception onboard for the benefit of US Defense Bonds. Noted speakers were John W. Snyder, the Secretary of the Treasury, and George C. Marshall, General of the Army. The day's events on board included a fashion show organized by Filene's Department Store.

The Purser's Staff of the Maiden Voyage

Dining Room Mural

On Monday, June 11th, 1951, the *Constitution* departed from Boston with over 300 guest-passengers aboard. One of them was a young actress-model named Grace Kelly. She was hired by American Export along with several others for press photography. General Marshall and his wife also made the overnight trip. At New York, American Export organized a thorough welcome. A Moran tugboat left Pier A at the Battery at 8:45 in the morning with reporters and photographers, newsreel and television men, and radio reporters. Some boarded the *Constitution* in the Lower Bay while others sailed with the tug to Pier 84, circling the liner en route. The *Constitution* arrived at her West 44th Street berth at exactly 11 o'clock; soon afterward, Mayor Impellitteri went aboard to extend the city's welcome greetings. Six other US-flag passenger ships were in port that same day: *the Washington, America, Uruguay, Veragua, Santa Margarita,* and *African Endeavor.*

Designer Henry Dreyfuss was among those who met with reporters welcoming the new liner. He noted, "The only difference between the interior design of these nautical twins are some paintings and other works of art, and the names of suites and a few public rooms. Apart from these, the passenger spaces on one ship are the same as on the other, from the 12 air-conditioned dog kennels on the Sports Deck to the auditorium eight decks below ... Having two ships to work with meant being able to order double quantities of everything ...This covered everything in the public rooms and general passenger spaces, from the soda fountain in the pool cafe to the piano in the tourist class bar. Since the design project included the numerous accessories aboard the ships, there were additional savings with such items as china-ware, glassware, ashtrays, blankets and even soap wrappers."

"The largest difference between the twins is the 40-foot mural in the first class dining room. In the *Constitution's* Riviera Restaurant, Lyonel Feininger's painting of a Mediterranean seaport covers the curved bulkhead. In the comparable Atlantic Restaurant on the *Independence,* there is a Joe Jones painting of Boston harbor as seen from the sea. Other changes include an exact copy of the United States Constitution on one ship and a replica of the Declaration of Independence on the other; exact scale models of the *USS Constitution* (OLD IRONSIDES) and the old time Navy frigate *USS Independence,* a 22-foot map mural by Allan Saalburg in the Oak Room on the *Constitution* and one by Henry Billings in the same room on the *Independence;* a replica of a Hercules figurehead in the Main Foyer of the *Constitution* and an American Indian figurehead on the *Independence;* and two sets of 40 miniature ship models, with each model in its own hand-blown bottle, in the Boat'n Bottle bars. In addition to these, none of the stateroom art (about 325 water colors, sketches, serigraphs, etc on each ship) is duplicated in the other."

Opened for public inspection and used for numerous tours, receptions, luncheons and dinners, the ship hosted a glamorous event, the Flag Day Preview Ball, held on Thursday night, June 14th. Over 1,000 guests including Gertrude Lawrence, Lillian Gish, Ilka Chase, Ruth Gordon, Lucille Lortel, Nanette Fabray and Yma Sumac attended the benefit, which raised $21,000 for the American National Theatre and Academy. They were greeted by actress Gloria Swanson and entertained by the Lester Lanin and Alexander Haas orchestras.

A sudden strike by three maritime unions delayed the *Constitution's* June 21st maiden voyage four days. 936 passengers were set to sail - 293 in first class, 385 in cabin class, and 258 in tourist class. By late evening of the strike's first day, Export had telephoned or telegraphed all passengers stating, "Intensive negotiations are still in progress. However, even if a favorable conclusion is reached promptly, the earliest possible departure would be Friday evening." In fact, the liner did not sail until Monday, June 25. Sensibly, her Mediterranean port calls were reduced so that she could resume her published schedule.

"We'd come across to New York from Oakland, California by train to catch the maiden voyage of the *Constitution*," recalled Carla Kimble, then an 11-year-old traveling with her family, "but once we reached New York, we learned of the strike that delayed the ship. We stayed in a hotel for 4 days, anxiously calling American Export Lines once or twice a day and watching the newspapers. Once we finally settled onboard, the adventure began. My parents chose cabin class because it was said to be much more fun. That first night, as we sailed out past the Statue of Liberty, we sang a song about the *Titanic*. Tourist class was quite different. They had plastic tablecloths, for example, and those highly publicized 'saltwater cascades' on deck were actually public showers. There were lots of Italian waiters working on the ship. The first night out, the stewards couldn't find the cribs. They searched every closet onboard. First and cabin class shared the nighttime entertainment throughout the trip. I remember that during the crossing, my mother was locked in her cabin bathroom for several hours because the door handle came off. She finally freed herself by using bobby pins. The broken door was part of the newness of the ship. Ronald Colman was onboard. Still a very famous actor, all of us kids knocked on his stateroom door and asked for his autograph. He always said 'yes'."

On her eastbound maiden trip, the *Constitution* maintained a speed of 24.62 knots and traveled from New York to Gibraltar in 5 days and 10 hours, Margaret Truman was among the 700 passengers returning on the westbound maiden voyage. On her next sailing, July 14th, the liner made a special call at Boston to take on 150 religious pilgrims bound for a tour of the sacred shrines of Spain. The group was led by Reverend Richard J. Cushing, Archbishop of Boston.

American Export was very pleased with both ships, their performances and strong demand for passage. Rumors persisted for almost a decade that the Company would build a third sister ship or one of slightly larger size.

Supposedly, plans were even drawn up, but never passed that point. A three-liner service would have been ideal, allowing for a weekly departure in each direction with the third vessel in transit, but that maritime dream was never to be. In 1960, American Export did acquire a third passenger ship, the *Atlantic.* It was, however, no sister ship to the *Constitution* or the *Independence.* The *Atlantic* was a small (18,000-ton) tourist class ship with only forty first class spaces, intended mostly for economy crossings and cruisings. It ran until 1967.

The Independence at Funchal, Madeira

LIST OF PASSENGERS

AMERICAN EXPORT LINES

"Business was booming for just about everything and everyone in the fifties," according to historian Jack Weatherford. "The American dollar was at its highest. Even a middle class family could afford a European vacation. Buying power was at its greatest. There were opportunities to see more of the world. Attitudes were more open, more international. Soldiers of the War, for example, had been overseas...Ships like the *Independence* and the *Constitution* could not have arrived at a better time....At the same time, America symbolized efficiency and achievement. We had won the War!...America was in triumph. It was the most modern place on earth. Ships, the great liners, were still the gangways to this modern world, to a new life. Europe was still devastated in the fifties. Bombed-out buildings remained in many cities, including London and Rome. Italy, for example, was still tattered and in shambles. Many wanted to turn away from the past and the suffering and the depravation. Big, new American ships like the *Independence* and the *Constitution* were like rays of sunshine. They were not just for tourists, the millionaires, and the businessmen, and the school teachers on holiday, but for those post-war, westbound immigrants. They were gangways — fast, efficient, totally comfortable bridges to the New World!"

En Route to Europe, With Streamers

The *Independence* and the *Constitution* were generally scheduled on three-week round trip voyages: New York to Gibraltar (changed to Algeciras in 1956), Cannes, Genoa and Naples. They carried exactly 1,000 passengers — 295 in first class, 375 in cabin class and 330 in tourist class. Minimum fares to Italy in the maiden year were $335 in first class, $260 in cabin and $205 in tourist. "They were great ships especially the first class accommodations," recalls Herb Maletz, assistant comptroller at American Export in New York City in those years. "They had fantastic wine cellars, for example, that were selected by Alexis Lecchine himself. There was French silver service and live music at dinner, and you could have a steak at 3 in the morning if you wanted. Everything was done with great style. The first ten to twelve years were very successful financially... We had lots of military officers and their families in first class. The enlisted men were in cabin class. We also had Italian immigrants going westbound in tourist class. And there were huge numbers of Catholic priests and nuns always coming and going. American Export always had good contacts with the Roman Catholic Church on both sides of the Atlantic."

Vito and Maria Cuocci, for example, emigrated from Naples to New York in 1955. "Even in tourist class, it was a world for us that we could not imagine. There was air conditioning, attentive service, plentiful food, Coca-Cola even. The ship was immaculate, sparkling. There were many other Italian immigrants as well. Like us, many selected the ship because it was a taste of America even before we landed. We felt as if we were already on American soil. I shall never forget the April morning as we came into New York harbor: the Statue of Liberty, the big buildings, all the boats in the harbor at work. That afternoon, after we cleared the immigration formalities, I looked back at the *Independence*. We will never forget that great, wonderful ship."

First class was, of course, much more glamorous. "There was a sign in our cabin aboard the *Constitution* that offered food twenty-four hours a day," recalls Reverend Neville Rucker. He crossed on the *Constitution* in 1954. "You could have a seven-course meal even at 3 in the morning, but the request was needed one-hour in advance. And so, one evening, I ordered

Waving Farewell

Circular Lounge, Designed by Henry Dreyfuss

escargot, French onion soup, pheasant and crepes suzettes. The pheasant was fixed in a casserole dish and it was quite authentic with a tail feather stuck in. It was carried very high on a tray by a very proper waiter. We left the ship at Gibraltar, did overland travel in Europe for 10 days and caught the *Constitution* on her return sailing to New York. It was terrific!"

Lew Gordon and his wife sailed aboard these ships on several occasions. "In first class on the *Independence* and the *Constitution*, it was usual to see 5 and 10 carat diamond rings at dinner. But when one woman wore a 47 carat diamond, it was called 'vulgar'. There were always Greek shipping magnates onboard. I remember Mrs. Goulandris, who wore jewels from the best shops in Paris and all of them at the same time! There were some evening activities, like dancing and horse racing and films, but otherwise you sat on deck all day long with little to do. It was very relaxing, very comfortable." First class also often included many celebrities from entertainment, sports, and politics.

Cardinal Cushing Putting On Deck

Cardinal Cushing Baptizing in the Ship's Pool

The following is a list of the of some of the celebrities who sailed aboard the *Independence* and the *Constitution* in the 1950's.

Jerry Lewis

Anthony Quinn

Richard Conti

Cardinal Cushing

Jinx Falkenberg

Irving Berlin

Alan Ladd

Cecil B. De Mille

Glenn Ford

Yvonne De Carlo

Gracie Fields

Rossano Brazzi

Allan Funt

Jimmy Hoffa

Sophie Tucker

Zachary Scott

Mae West

Ralph Bellamy

John D. Roosevelt

Mary Pickford

Walt Disney

Ernest Hemingway

Carroll O'Connor

Jack Carson

Estes Kefauver

Joe Di Maggio

Lou Costello

The Three Stooges

Gina Lolabrigida

Katherine Hepburn

Edward Everett Horton

Art Buchwald

Jack Dempsey

John Cabot Lodge

Elia Kazan

Walter Winchell

Peter Ustinov

Mae West on Board with a Friend

"On several other occasions, we had Ibn Saud, the King of Saudi Arabia," remembers Herb Maletz. "The ships were diverted several times to either meet or drop him off at Casablanca. He was an extraordinary passenger. He gave $1,000 tips as well as gold Rolex watches to the staff. Even a simple bow from a steward warranted a tip, perhaps a $100 bill. A treasurer with a small leather case followed the King everywhere onboard."

The Three Stooges Clown with Bob Harrow

R. FLEURY
A.G.E.N.T. CANNES

GENERAL PASSENGER AGENTS
FOR
AMERICAN EXPORT LINES, INC.

BUILDING DU CASINO
PH. 932-80 & 939-84

N Y OFFICE ENright 9-0561

Bob Harrow
News Photographer

S. S CONSTITUTION
PIER 84   N. RIVER
NEW YORK, N. Y.

SWARTHMORE 2-2700

SUN LANE SHOP

SEYMOUR O. SUSSMAN

CARE OF:
AMERICAN EXPORT LINES, INC.
RIVER & FIRST STS., HOBOKEN, N. J.

Ernest Hemmingway — The Old Man and the Sea

Anthony Quinn and the Atlantic Ocean

"Give 'Em Hell Harry" Tours the Ship

During a January 1957 crossing to New York, King Ibn Saud and his entourage of 69 were aboard the *Constitution.* The *New York Times* reported, "Saudi Arabia's exchequer expended an estimated $20,000 in tips and gifts during the 9-day crossing from Naples. Captain James LaBelle was given a gold watch with an enamel miniature of the King on the dial. The six-man guard of United States Marines who traveled on the liner were also presented with gold watches. A watch was also given to Emilio Royira, the King's cabin steward ... The King and 15 of his party left the brightly-lit *Constitution* during the predawn darkness in New York's Lower Bay and transferred to the US Coast Guard tugboat *Tuckahoe.* The tug then headed for the Navy frigate *Willis A. Lee*, which was waiting about a mile off. The frigate flashed a 21-gun salute as the King arrived. The *Lee* then steamed up to the Hudson River as 8 Navy destroyers formed a guard of honor before landing the monarch and his party at Pier 45 at the foot of West 10th Street in Greenwich Village."

In December, 1955, and January, 1956, the *Constitution* featured in several episodes of the popular "I Love Lucy" show. The sequence began with Ricky landing a European tour for his band and Lucy's madcap attempts to raise the money to accompany him by an illegal raffle. The first episode ended with Ricky securing a booking for the band on a transatlantic ship so that Lucy, Ethel, and Fred could have free passage. Episode two centered on Lucy's attempts to secure a birth certificate so that she could get a passport. Episode three found Lucy sleeping through a crucial interview to get her passport. Episode four was set on sailing day. Lucy rushed off the ship to say one last goodbye to her son, missed the sailing (because her skirt was stuck in a bicycle chain) and was finally lowered to the deck from a helicopter. In the last episode, the romantic atmosphere of the ship made Lucy lonely.

(Ricky was always busy with the band.) Lucy locked herself and Ricky in the stateroom, only to discover that he had planned a romantic evening for the two of them. In her frantic attempts to get out, Lucy got her head stuck in the porthole. The evening ended with acetylene torches. In none of these episodes was Lucille Ball or Desi Arnez actually on the ship. Designers measured and photographed the public areas and staterooms; they then created accurate sets in Hollywood. All of the exteriors, however, are actual shots of the *Constitution.*

In 1956, Twentieth Century-Fox decided to remake the 1938 film *Love Affair*, retitled *An Affair To Remember.* Cary Grant and Deborah Kerr starred; almost half of the story took place aboard a New York-bound ocean liner. That same year, Fox designer John Dapper and film editor Lyman Hollowell returned from a European vacation aboard the *Constitution.* They boarded at Naples. "It was a tense voyage in ways," recalled Dapper. "We had a US Navy sub escort in the western Mediterranean because of the Suez Crisis. But I remember her as a very pretty ship with attractive passenger spaces.

Harry Likes What He Sees Touring the Ship

Harry and Bess

CLAUDIA WELLS (LONZETTI) RECALLS A MEMORABLE SAILING.

"I SAILED ON THE SS CONSTITUTION, FROM NEW YORK TO NAPLES, MARCH 13-MARCH 22, 1958. MY BEST FRIEND, ANNETTE CONTINENZA, AND MYSELF... WERE NINETEEN YEARS OLD. HER MOTHER, JOSEPHINE CONTINEZA, AND TWELVE YEAR OLD SISTER, KATHLEEN CONTINEZA, COMPLETED OUR PARTY. THE JOURNEY WAS TO VISIT THEIR RELATIVES IN ROME AND THEN MEET AND DRIVE WITH OTHER RELATIVES TO FRANKFURT, GERMANY WHERE THEY WERE STATIONED WITH THE MILITARY. WE WERE IN EUROPE FOR THREE MONTHS. WE RETURNED ON THE SS UNITED STATES. FOR MY FRIEND AND MYSELF THE SAILING WAS OUR ENTRANCE INTO ADULTHOOD. IT WAS THE MOST MAGICAL TIME. WE MET FIVE YOUNG ITALIAN MEN FROM HOBOKEN, NEW JERSEY WHO WERE RETURNING TO ITALY TO VISIT. ONE WAS RETURNING TO BE MARRIED. WE HUNG OUT AS A GROUP, PLAYING CARDS, DANCING, WALKING THE DECKS, SINGING ITALIAN SONGS, STAYING UP ALL NIGHT AND GOING TO BREAK-FAST, TALKING, LAUGHING AND JUST HAVING FUN. WE CRIED AND SOBBED IN NAPLES WHEN WE HAD TO SAY GOODBYE TO BOTH THE BOYS AND THE SS CONSTITUTION. MY LOVE OF TRAVELING STARTED WITH THAT VOYAGE."

Claudia Wells

Captain's Dinner, Last Night on Board, Claudia & Friends

The Wells Party at Embarkation

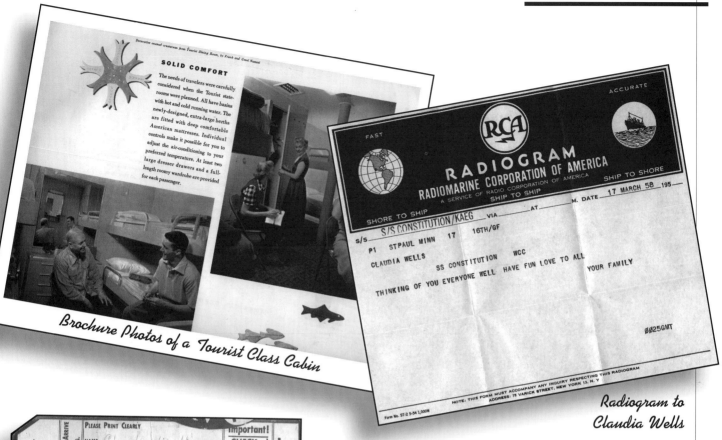

SOLID COMFORT

The needs of travelers were carefully considered when the Tourist state-rooms were planned. All have basins with hot and cold running water. The newly-designed, extra-large berths are fitted with deep comfortable American mattresses. Individual controls make it possible for you to adjust the air-conditioning to your preferred temperature. At least two large dresser drawers and a full-length roomy wardrobe are provided for each passenger.

Brochure Photos of a Tourist Class Cabin

Radiogram to Claudia Wells

Luggage Tag

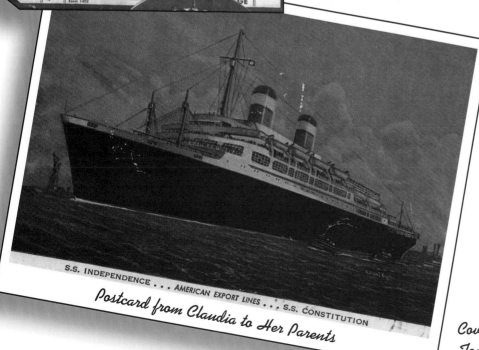

Postcard from Claudia to Her Parents

Cover of Tourist Class Brochure

An Old Salt and A Modern Ship, Madeira, 1958

I took lots of photos and slides of her. Ironically, when we returned to Los Angeles, we were assigned by Fox to *An Affair to Remember*. They already selected the *Constitution* for the film and so it was very coincidental. Actually, the film was already in early production. We worked in reverse, however. We made the complete sets for Deborah Kerr's New York apartment and other City sets first. Then we did the ship. We used my slides, which were enlarged to great sizes and all of which were made into 8x10 glossies. We also had a fantastic research library as well in those days at Fox. Parts of the pictures of the *Constitution* were enlarged right down to doorways, even to the head of a screw. We kept enlarging. Everything had to be authentic. We built whole sections of the *Constitution*, such as the lido deck and pool, to complete accuracy. I remember that once it started, the picture had to move quickly. Cary Grant received premium pay in those days. Otherwise, if there were delays, he would receive triple pay. He had a strong agent and one of the greatest contracts in Hollywood. Typically, of course, once our work was completed, we moved on to another film. There were so many in those days, but I shall always remember the amazing coincidence involving the *Constitution*."

Former President Harry Truman and his wife Bess returned from a European vacation aboard the *Constitution* in the early summer of 1958. On the Fourth of July, the President addressed the 1,500 passengers and crew. His speech, entitled "The Effect of the Declaration of Independence and the Constitution of the United States on the World," was carried on the ship's public address system to every part of the vessel including the engine room.

Maritime historian and photographer Everett Viez and his wife were passengers aboard the *Independence* in 1959, sailing on one of those three-week

Mediterranean cruises. "The blue Mediterranean was not calm that trip," recalled Viez, "but the *Independence* proved to be an excellent 'sea boat'. She was a good-sized ship, but never a crowded ship. She was about 80% full on our sailing. She was also an immaculate ship. She had conservative yet modern interiors, impeccable food and top-notch service. She also had the best prime ribs of beef on the Atlantic run."

Beginning in 1953-54, these American Export sisters had competition on the New York-Mediterranean run from the new luxury ships of the Italian Line, the *Andrea Doria* and her sister, *Cristoforo Colombo*. Herb Maletz recalls, "We were equal, if not better in some ways to the Italian Line at that time. When the *Independence* and *Constitution* were conceived in 1948-49, John Slater, the financial genius who was then president of American Export, wanted big liners. But he insisted that such three class ships must also be like cruise ships. He believed that there would be passengers making the round voyage, a three-week cruise, New York to the western Mediterranean and back again. And so, a man brought over from San Francisco's Matson Line invented 'Sunlane Cruises' for American Export. These were voyages of 21-23 days and where the ports were varied some-times. We'd call occasionally at Casablanca, Malaga, Funchal or Las Palmas. We were always testing, trying to increase our appeal."

Much more serious competition was to come from air travel. Technical developments moved from military to civilian aircraft steadily through the 1950's, making planes faster, quieter, and more comfortable.

Stopping in Haifa

THE PARTHENON, ATHENS

Luncheon

AMALFI

Luncheon

BEACH, CANNES

Luncheon

BRALTAR

PHILIP GENDREAU, N. Y.

Luncheon

THE ALHAMBRA, GRANADA

PHILIP GENDREAU, N. Y.

Luncheon

PISA AND THE LEANING TOWER

THE OLD APPIAN WAY

Luncheon

Luncheon

AMERICAN EXPORT LINES

Dinner Menus

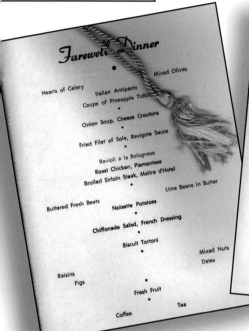

Farewell Dinner

Mixed Olives

Hearts of Celery
Italian Antipasto
Coupe of Pineapple Tidbits

Onion Soup, Cheese Croutons

Fried Filet of Sole, Ravigote Sauce

Ravioli a la Bolognese
Roast Chicken, Piemontese
Broiled Sirloin Steak, Maitre d'Hotel

Lima Beans in Butter

Buttered Fresh Beets
Noisette Potatoes

Chiffonade Salad, French Dressing

Biscuit Tortoni

Mixed Nuts
Dates

Raisins
Figs

Fresh Fruit

Coffee   Tea

Get-together Dinner

APPETIZERS	Sliced Egg, Piemonteise	Parma Ham	Sardines di Nantes
	Green Olives	Supreme of Fresh Fruit, Maraschino	Spring Onions
	Iced Table Celery		Stuffed Tomato Surprise
SOUP	Fresh Vegetable Soup, Cultivateur	Consomme Pastina	Consomme Florentine
FISH		Poached Tranche of Swordfish, Choisy	
ENTREE	Home Made Ravioli with Tomato Sauce and Parmesan Cheese		
	Braised Beef a la Mode with German Pancake		
	Fresh Vegetable Plate with Poached Egg		
ROAST	Roast Philadelphia Capon, Giblet Sauce, Celery Dressing, Spiced Peach		
FROM THE GRILL	Grilled Sugar-Cured Ham with Pineapple Ring Glace		
COLD DISHES	Roast Chicken, Sliced Tomatoes		Pate Maison
	Salami or Mortadella, Milanaise	Assorted Cold Cuts, Potato Salad	
	Truffles Galantine of Duckling		
VEGETABLES	New Peas and Carrots au Beurre		Corn on the Cob
POTATOES	Mousseline	Hashed Brown	
SALAD	Mixed Green		Fondante
Dressing	Lorenzo	Boston and Tomato	Escarole
		French	Roquefort
DESSERT	Mocha Cake	Strawberry Bavarian Cream	
	Cream Puff Chantilly	Peach Melba	Chocolate Sundae
	Chocolate, Vanilla, Pistachio or Coffee Ice Cream		Coupe St. Jacques
		Lemon, Raspberry or Orange Sherbet	
CHEESE	Liederkranz	Cream	Roquefort	Limburger
		Crackers		Toast
		Fresh Fruit Basket		
		Iced Coffee	Coffee	Iced Tea

CHARLES REGIS, Chief Steward   (c)   RUDOLPH KRESSERVICH, Chef de Cuisine

Armistice Day Dinner

ICED TABLE CELERY   BLACK AND QUEEN OLIVES   GARDEN RADISHES

SUPREME OF FRESH FRUIT CUP AU MARASCHINO   CANAPE ROUGE ET NOIR

DOUBLE CONSOMME ROYAL EN TASSE
CREAM OF CHICKEN, ARGENTEUIL
COLD CONSOMME MADRILENE

GOLDEN BROOK TROUT SAUTE WITH CUCUMBER DORIA

BROILED NEW YORK SIRLOIN STEAK, MAITRE D'HOTEL BUTTER SAUCE
ROAST MARYLAND TOM TURKEY, CHESTNUT DRESSING
GIBLET SAUCE, CRANBERRY JELLY

ASPARAGUS TIPS, GREEN PEAS A LA FRANCAISE, CHATEAU POTATOES

LEMON SHERBET

BELGIAN ENDIVE WITH LORENZO DRESSING

FRESH STRAWBERRY TART   AMERICAN CUP   BUTTER COOKIES
FROZEN CREAM PUFF, CHOCOLATE SAUCE   BLUEBERRY SUNDAE

FRESH DATES   CLUSTER RAISINS   MIXED NUTS   AFTER DINNER MINTS
CHEESE VARIES   TOASTED CRACKERS
FRESH FRUIT BASKET

CAFE NOIR

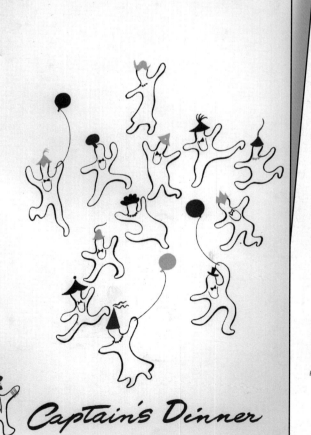

Captain's Dinner
AMERICAN EXPORT LINES

Captain's Dinner

BAKED CAPECOD OYSTER CASINO
FRESH FRUIT CUP, RAFRAICHI au KUMMEL
FRESH MAINE LOBSTER WITH PARISIENNE SAUCE
ICED TABLE CELERY   RIPE AND QUEEN OLIVES

VELOUTES EGYPTIENNE, au CROUTONS
CONSOMME DOUBLE EN TASSE, NATIONAL

WHOLE DOVER SOLE SAUTE DORIA WITH CUCUMBER, MAITRE D'HOTEL

GRILLED FILET MIGNON WITH FRESH MUSHROOM SAUCE
ASPARAGUS TIPS, FRENCH STRING BEANS AU BEURRE, FONDANTE POTATOES

RASPBERRY SHERBET WITH NABISCO WAFERS

GLAZED SMITHFIELD HAM, CHAMPAGNE SAUCE
CANDIED SWEET POTATOES
GARDEN SPINACH, SWEET BUTTER

BELGIAN ENDIVE, LORENZO DRESSING

PETITS FOURS GLACE   LALLAROOCK PUNCH   AMERICAN CUP
FROZEN CREAM PUFF, CHOCOLATE SAUCE   FRESH PEACH TART
INDEPENDENCE BOMBE, ZABACLIONE SAUCE   BLUEBERRY SUNDAE

FRESH DATES   CLUSTER RAISINS   MIXED NUTS   AFTER DINNER MINTS
CHEESE VARIES   TOASTED CRACKERS
FRESH FRUIT BASKET

CAFE NOIR

Airlines' share of transatlantic traffic rose steadily; by 1957, it equaled the number of passengers carried by all steamship lines. A year later, in October 1958, commercial jet service to and from Europe began. Within six months, the airlines had captured two-thirds of all transatlantic travelers, but American Export, like many others, still saw some bright, profitable years ahead. In the summer of 1958, the *Independence* and the *Constitution* consistently arrived at New York better than 90% full.

Indeed, American Export was concerned, but not enough to curtail plans or make drastic changes. Accordingly, the *Constitution* was sent to the giant Newport News shipyard in Virginia in early January, 1959. Ambitious plans called for "rolling" the wheelhouse, bridge wings and navigation rooms 21 feet forward and 8 ½ feet up to allow room for four new verandah suites and fourteen new double cabins with private bathrooms on the Sun Deck, plus 38 new cabins on the Promenade Deck.

In Dock, Naples

Independence in New York, 1958

The renovations added a new
Solarium and a new writing room and card room.
Several lounges as well as the Boat 'n' Bottle Bar received new furnishings.

Maritime reporter Walter Hamshar wrote extensively on the project. "The principle of the inclined plane, used by Egypt's pyramid builders, was put in use again by the Newport News shipyard in moving a 320,000 pound bridge section of the liner *Constitution* to a new position. The gigantic steel section was mounted on skids resting on an inclined plane made by setting eight 18-inch "I" beams at an angle of about 30 degrees under the section to be moved. The section was then burned loose and hauled by four huge geared chain falls operated by men pulling chains through the falls. The big section, the equivalent of a two-story house of 11 rooms, moved inch by inch up the beams until it was 21 feet forward and 8½ feet higher than its original position. The moving took 9 hours."

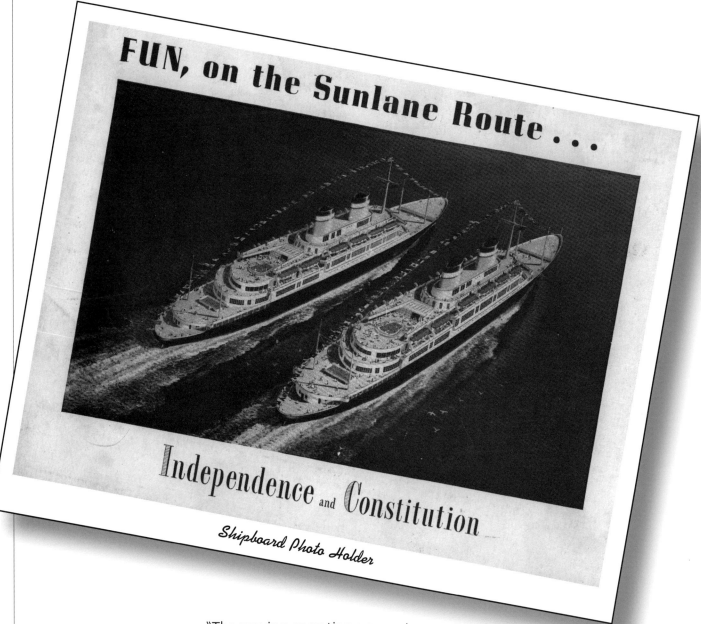

FUN, on the Sunlane Route . . .

Independence and Constitution

Shipboard Photo Holder

"The moving operation was part of a $6.7 million program to add accommodations to the *Constitution* and the *Independence*," concluded Hamshar. "The yard is working around the clock to complete the conversion of the *Constitution* by the first week in March. The *Independence* will follow. It was the first time that the ancient principle has been used for such a project. Generally, the movement of a ship section to another position is done by hoisting it with giant cranes working in tandem. The *Constitution* section was too big for cranes at the dry-dock."

On March 1st, returning to service, the *Constitution* made headline news. Just outside the entrance to New York harbor, she rammed and cut in two the Norwegian oil tanker *Jalanta*. "The *Constitution's* master was going too fast and cut corners because he had a pressing appointment in New York City," said Herb Maletz. "She had a large cut in her port bow section and so had to go directly to Bethlehem Steel's shipyard at 56th Street in Brooklyn. The repairs were expensive. The two sections of the *Jalanta* were also given over to Bethlehem Steel, but to their plant in Hoboken. They were later welded together and the ship repaired fully, but it all cost American Export millions and with lots of poor publicity. We were the villains."

The two liners were repainted with white hulls in 1960 and began to spend part of the winter off-season months in lay-up at the Company's three-pier cargo terminal at Hoboken, New Jersey. Sometimes they would be idle together, lying alongside the 900-foot Pier B, "They would be in Hoboken for several weeks for wet dock repairs, maintenance and for their Coast Guard inspections," remembers Herb Maletz, "American Export's engineering staff was located in offices at the Hoboken terminal." These layups also reflected decreasing passenger demand, a theme we will explore in the next chapter.

At the opening of the 1960's, all transatlantic passenger lines faced grim prospects. Competition from airliners was serious and getting more so. Through the mid-fifties, propeller planes competed for the transatlantic trade, but these airplanes were slow, uncomfortable, noisy, expensive, and made several stops. In 1958, however, British Overseas Airways began daily jet flights across the Atlantic. Other carriers, including Pan American, quickly replaced their prop planes with jets.

Norton Bain and his wife sailed from New York to Genoa aboard the *Constitution* in September, 1958. "It was said to be the roughest crossing of that ship's career," said Bain. "At Gibraltar, we passed the *Independence*, which was going westbound. We felt sorry for her passengers. We heard that it was even worse than what we experienced. There were stories that several passengers had broken arms or broken legs."

Constitution, painted white, in New York Harbor, 1960

The following month, the Bains planned to return to the United States on Pan American Airways regular propeller service. In London, however, they saw an ad in the *London Times* for the inaugural westbound flight of Pan Am's new jetliner service. "We changed our reservations to that special flight ... When we arrived at London Airport, Maxim's Restaurant of Paris was catering a huge party. It was very gala. There were lots of officials and dignitaries present. A fog delayed the actual take off by two hours so the party just continued. There was also a slight seating problem so they put both of us in first class. There was fine food and an open bar all the way across the Atlantic. We stopped at Gander in Newfoundland to refuel and then went onward to

New York. In all, the flight took 8 $\frac{1}{2}$ hours as compared to the 13 $\frac{1}{2}$ by prop plane."

"The jet revolutionized travel. The ocean liner as we knew it was finished. It was all a matter of time," concluded Norton Bain. "Those earlier 14-hour flights had been exhausting and noisy and always hit storms. Now, the jets were much more quiet and flew at greater speeds and above the storms. There were many Pan Am executives with us in first class on that inaugural flight. For all of us onboard, we realized that the jet would change travel forever."

Drawing of Family Boarding The Independence

Ocean liners quickly lost their business travelers, the thousands of wholesale buyers who went to Europe for clothes and wine, woolens and machinery, and the thousands more who went to sell wire and farm machinery, oil and wheat. For them, a week at sea was a waste of time.

The Last of The Four Aces, 1963

What remained were immigrants returning to visit relatives, families "doing" Europe, mothers and their children joining men working in Europe, adventurous teenagers going abroad, military taking up assignments, and State Department personnel.

Shipping lines responded to the loss of business travelers and declining passenger numbers in several ways. There was some consolidation. For example, another American ship owner, the Isbrandtsen Company, gained controlling interest in American Export. Many lines simply retired older, inefficient ships. American Export, for example, retired the last of the post-war "Four Aces", the *Exeter* and *Excalibur*, in 1964. Even relatively modern ships were sold off; the *America*, for example, went to Greek owners in 1964. Other lines sought less competitive markets, where air travel was still in its infancy. Most companies looked for ways to capitalize on the benefits of ocean travel: the relaxed pace, the luxury, the chance to socialize, the gourmet food. American Export Lines was no exception. The line's 1962 brochure asked "Why just get there?" and offered the alternative, "Cruise there", and absorb "fascinating ports ...enchanting islands ...enjoy leisurely sightseeing and shopping" and offered these places "on your way to your destination ...which cost you not a penny more." The literature offered "the luxury of gracious service ...superb cuisine ...carefully organized entertainment ...air conditioning ...private bath with tub or shower ...outdoor pools ...traditional deck sports ...meeting attractive new friends."

American Export's position in the transatlantic trade was somewhat better than many competitors'. The line was subsidized by the United States Government (though

Brochure Cover, 1962

other lines also had subsidies); more importantly, the design of the *Independence* and the *Constitution* included some consideration for cruising, rather than purely scheduled crossings. The ships, for example, were not as completely divided by class as some others; some stairways, for example, connected the top decks with some of the lower decks. Also, the routes required by the government were more likely to appeal to potential cruise passengers. The New York - Genoa route was far south of the stormy corridor directly to Southampton, a feature the line vigorously promoted with its "Sunlane" motto.

Even in the 1950's, American Export experimented with some "cruises". Seasonally, they added several ports of call to the normal run, usually in the Mediterranean: Tripoli, Alexandria, Haifa, or Istanbul. Once, they sold a "Great Cruise" with transits of the Suez Canal, passage down the west coast of India, and stops at Bombay and Colombo. In the early 1960's, all sailings became "cruises" of slightly over twenty days with excursions in various Mediterranean

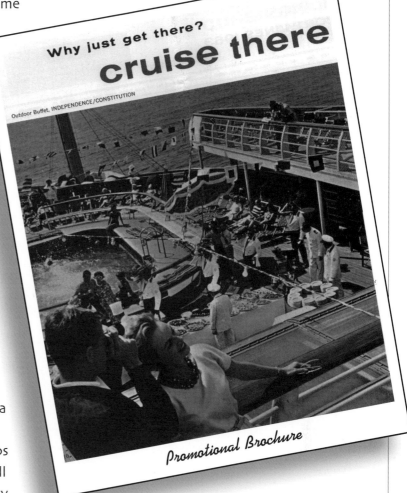

Why just get there? cruise there

Outdoor Buffet, INDEPENDENCE/CONSTITUTION

Promotional Brochure

ports. Passengers could also "modify" the cruise by coming back on a later sailing of either vessel. A typical itinerary began in New York and included the Canary Islands or Madeira, Gibraltar, Naples, the French Riviera, Spain and North Africa. Alternate ports in those years included Casablanca, Palma, and Messina. Promotional literature advertised the "low, low price" of $629 - $800 for cabin class (with substantial discounts for non-summer travel) and $802 - $3800 for first class. (With inflation adjustment, these rates were, in fact, substantially cheaper than rates commanded by the ship all through the 1950's.)

Nevertheless, passenger and embarkation lists show that the idea of a "cruise" to Europe and back was actually slow to catch on. Only a small percent of passengers stayed onboard for a whole voyage, New York to New York. For example, on the September 6, 1961 sailing from New York, only about 50 of the roughly 300 first class passengers took the full "cruise". Most treated the trip as transportation to Europe. American Export recognized this situation

Welcome Aboard

Poolside

and responded with combined air/sea packages, which allowed vacationers to have a week at sea, a little time in Europe, and still return in two weeks. Passengers found this option more appealing after TWA replaced their slower propeller overnight European service with modern jets in 1962.

Sailings always allowed time for tours ashore at ports of call, "arranged so that passengers will be able to see - conveniently, pleasantly, and comfortably - the principal points of historic, scenic, and unusual interest and capture the color, charm, and romance of the Mediterranean". For example, the November 13, 1964 sailing listed thirteen possible shore tours including Gibraltar, Palma, Naples, and Cannes. Typical was this afternoon and evening expedition from Casablanca; it cost $14.50 per person.

"Motor coaches will drive through Casablanca and north along the main coast road to Rabat, capital of the Kingdom of Morocco. On arrival view the King's Palace from the outside, guarded by red-uniformed soldiers. Continue through the French section of the city with its palm-lined boulevards past the tomb of Marshall Lyautey to the Tower of Hassan. This imposing structure is all that remains of the Grand Mosque, destroyed by an earthquake. Visits are made to the Medina and the "Souks" - a colorful Moroccan shopping district. Dinner will be served at Rabat, after which return to Casablanca.

Shopping facilities: Ornate and heavy pieces of jewelry, tooled leather, hassocks, hand bags, traveling bags, slippers, change purses, pillows and many other items. Be sure that leather articles do not have any odor.

Perfumes: The pungent perfumes you will find here are unlike any from Paris, but lovely in their own exotic way."

Itinerary/Passenger List, 1961

THE GREAT GLOBES

...DURING THE WAR,
A REQUEST CAME FROM WASHINGTON
FOR FOUR GLOBES OF THE WORLD
MORE THAN THIRTEEN FEET IN CIRCUMFERENCE
AND REVOLVABLE IN ANY DIRECTION.
ALUMINUM BEING UNAVAILABLE,
THE GLOBES WERE CONSTRUCTED OF LAMINATED HOOPS
OF CHERRYWOOD, DOWELED EVERY SIX INCHES
TO PREVENT EXPANSION AND CONTRACTION,
AND COVERED WITH DETAILED MAPS OF THE WORLD
DRAWN BY THE NATIONAL GEOGRAPHIC SOCIETY.
TO PERMIT THE GLOBES TO TURN EASILY,
WE FIRST CONSIDERED A POOL OF MERCURY
IN WHICH THEY WOULD FLOAT, BUT THIS WAS DISCARDED
BECAUSE MERCURY IS POISONOUS.
EXPERIMENT PROVED THAT A "CUP" OF HARD RUBBER BALLS
WORKING AGAINST STEEL BALLS
GAVE THE SAME EASY ACTION.
ONLY ON THE DAY OF DELIVERY
DID OUR "CLIENTS" BECOME KNOWN TO US -
PRESIDENT ROOSEVELT AND PRIME MINISTER CHURCHILL,
MARSHAL STALIN, AND THE U. S. ARMY.
YEARS LATER, WHEN WE WERE DOING
THE INDEPENDENCE AND THE CONSTITUTION,
THESE GLOBES WERE REPRODUCED
WITH THE U.S. ARMY'S PERMISSION
AND TODAY OCCUPY PROMINENT POSITIONS
IN THE LIBRARIES ABOARD THESE VESSELS.
THE MOTION OF THE SHIP AT SEA DEMANDED A MORE
SECURE FASTENING THAN OUR RUBBER-BALL BEARINGS,
AND THE GLOBES ARE HELD
IN THE TRADITIONAL GIMBALS.

HENRY DREYFUSS,
DESIGNING FOR PEOPLE (1955)

Henry Dreyfuss' Sketch of The Globe

THE GREAT GLOBES
DISAPPEARED FROM BOTH
THE INDEPENDENCE AND
THE CONSTITUTION
DURING LAY UP
IN THE 1970s.

THEIR CURRENT WHEREABOUTS
ARE UNKNOWN.

Much admired are the globes of 50-inch diameter which stand in the Map Corridor of each ship. Especially made for the ships, they are similar to those used by the General Staff during the war.

Promotional Brochure, 1962

The Governors' Conference, 1968

In the middle years of the 1960's, American Export's one solid passenger market on the transatlantic run was government and military personnel. As one of the last American transatlantic carriers (and recipient of subsidy), the line was required for government travel. Gus de Chelle, a passenger on a New York - Genoa - New York sailing from those years recalls:

"...since both boats were heavily subsidized by the U.S. Government, both were extensively used by the State Department and military people when going or coming from European Assignments. I hear it was a nightmare to decide who got the better cabins as all this was done according to rank. Who is higher, a general ...or a returning ambassador? As you can imagine, there were extensive class distinctions among the government people - especially the wives! As a civilian, I found it most amusing, and as a young man it was fun to chase the unattended govt. girls."

In 1961, American Export successfully petitioned the US Government for permission to use both the *Constitution* and the *Independence* for cruises outside their scheduled European runs. The *Independence* began her winter Caribbean cruises on January 18, 1962; she took passengers on a second short cruise to Bermuda in July of that year.

Nancy and Ronnie at the Governor's Conference, 1967

Discharge Papers, 1965

(In 1963, American Export Line began sending its *Atlantic* on fourteen day Caribbean "beachcomber" cruises.) The company also promoted the ships for conferences and conventions. Group rates made it competitive with hotels and resorts for such meetings. Ford Motor Company was a frequent customer. In 1966, for example, Lincoln-Mercury Division chartered the *Independence*; dealers viewed the coming models while they sailed in the Caribbean. In 1967, the annual Governor's Conference was held aboard the *Independence*. Many well known politicians were aboard; Bob Harrow, onboard photographer, photographed them, including presidential hopeful Nelson Rockefeller and the Governor of California, Ronald Reagan. The ship garnered brief media attention when a confidential memo on issues in the Vietnam War to the Johnson White House was delivered mistakenly to Reagan.

In those years, sixteen-year-old Michael Shernoff dreamed of going to sea, seeing far-off lands and, most of all, sailing aboard one of the great American ocean liners. In 1967, his dreams came true when he joined American Export Lines as a part time crew member, sailing during the summertime and during school holidays.

The Boat'n'Bottle Bar, 1960's

"I went to Pier 84 in June 1967 on my first assignment," he recalled, "but boarded the wrong ship. I walked aboard the *Constitution*, but only to be told that I was assigned to the *Atlantic*, which was, in an unusual occasion, actually berthed at the next pier, United States Lines' Pier 86. The *Independence* shared 84 with her sistership. I did not sail on the *Constitution* until that December, on the 12-day Christmas cruise from New York to Martinique, Barbados, Antigua, San Juan and St. Thomas."

"I was hired for a job called 'glory hole,' which meant making beds for the crew," recalled Shernoff. "But it lasted for only four hours before I became a night porter. I used to mop the solarium from I AM until 8 AM. But you could stop for a full breakfast at 3 AM. The food was, of course, fabulous. I really wanted to be a waiter, however. I had learned about food the summer before while sailing in the *Atlantic*. American Export did not have really sophisticated menus, but instead good, solid food. When I finally became a waiter on the *Constitution*, I used to inquire about all the menu items while I polished the silverware. I remember asking, 'What is wiener schnitzel?' I would spend about twenty minutes asking and learning before each meal. A fabulous waiter named Freddy Martin taught me a great deal. He taught me always to anticipate the passengers' needs such as filling the iced water glasses, putting out the celery and olives, have the rolls and bread ready, and even to place fresh books of matches on the table. It was a rule that the better waiters got the better tips, and anticipation made for a better waiter. Of course, as a waiter, you had to tip some of your fellow

Sea Island Club, 1960's

workers, such as the cooks, the pantry people and even the bakers. Each pantry station had a tip box. As waiters, we had 6 passengers for each sitting, but no busboy. We worked three meals a day —- breakfast, lunch and the first sitting of dinner —- seven days a week. The base pay back in 1968 was $343.90 a month. The second sitting of dinner was considered overtime, which was rated at $2.04 an hour. Consequently, one month I earned as much as $480. We also earned overtime by serving afternoon tea and midnight buffet and for polishing glassware. Of course, holidays like the Fourth of July were overtime. As waiters, we helped one another, especially in the dining room. We rotated in something we called 'a hustle'. Two waiters shared twelve passengers and therefore it seemed that there was continuous service. We had some personalities like George Meany, Alice Moran [of the well known New York tugboat family] and actor Jerry Van Dyke. We dined after second sitting. We would reset a few tables just for us. We drank the leftover wines and always over-ordered the special desert."

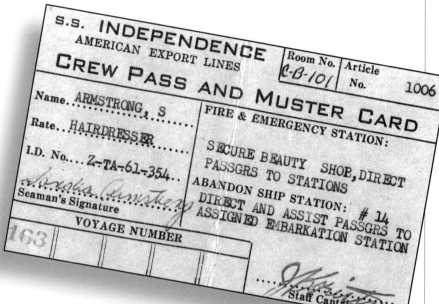

Crew Pass,
March 20, 1962

"There were lots of college kids working on the *Constitution* during the summers and school breaks," concluded Shernoff. "All needed some kind of 'connection' to work such a ship, either through the Company itself or through the unions. It certainly beat working the 'Borscht Belt' or in an office mailroom. We lived four or six to a cabin that had metal cabinets and lockers, and public toilets and showers along the corridor. Movies were shown and, of course, there was lots of gambling. There were always lots of attempts to meet girls. The tourist class bar was the favorite spot. I remember once when a group of guys, who were actually expert swimmers in college, swam from the beach at Cannes to the ship at anchor. They were heavily disciplined for this. Safety was a very high priority onboard the *Constitution*. The boat and the fire drills were done with great seriousness. The health of the crew members was also a major concern. Every crew member was examined by the Company doctor at least once a year. The ship itself was always very clean, immaculate actually. I remember the kitchens as being spotless aluminum from end to end. Ships like the *Constitution* actually took on the personality of their master. I remember one captain

The Jean Harlow Eyes, 1968

who ran a very tight ship, but who was beloved as well. While it was glamorous work in many ways, it was also hard work. In 1968, we knew the end was coming. I was to do a winter cruise on the *Independence*, but it was canceled just two weeks before the scheduled sailing. The ship was laid-up. The crew, especially the older members, were very bitter. It was, of course, the end of an era, a great era."

Neither cruising nor conferences solved the basic problems: passengers increasingly choose air travel over ocean travel. A typical passenger list from the late 1960's shows fewer than 200 first class passengers, down from over 300 at the beginning of the decade. By 1967, American Export Line was losing more than five million dollars a year, despite government subsidies. Desperate times called for radical measures. The Line retained Robert Miles Runyan and Associates, a leading design firm, to "modernize" the *Independence* to attract a younger "hip" clientele. With limited budget, the new decorations devolved to paint and wall treatments, fabrics and carpets. Nevertheless, the effect was radical. The ship came out of a two month dry dock in April, 1968, in full psychedelic colors. Passageways, formerly white, were now vibrant orange, yellow, and red. A foyer emerged with a yellow and blue zebra stripe pattern; large sculpture in the lobby appeared in painted metallic silver. A giant poster of a diver now hung over the pool, with the "splash" painted on the bottom of the pool. Pop art shouted from the walls of most of the public areas. Running out of money, the designers acquired huge circus posters, cut them to size and had a paperhanger mount them in the stairwells. Still to come was the most famous (or infamous) change. Runyan and Associates presented several exterior paint plans for identifying the ship as modern and "hip". One was George Washington with red stars and a blue whale; another was a vast American flag; yet another was a huge champagne bottle with the cork popping. What ultimately went on the entire side of the Independence was a half sun with rays rising all the way to the stacks and spreading out most of the length of the ship. On the sun was painted a pair of eyes graced with prominent eyebrows - supposed to be Jean Harlow's - looking forward. The ship was instantly identifiable, though the Italians identified the design as the "evil eye". The outside paint job lasted only six months, but was the prototype for many later total exterior paintings - of airliners, boats, buildings, and buses.

While the *Independence* tried new design to attract new passengers, the *Constitution* tried one-class service, special arrangements for golfers, low-calorie menus, and celebrity entertainment. The *Independence* offered a plan in which the cruise did not include meals; food was additional on a pay-as-you-go basis. The price started at $98 for a seven-day cruise. The idea did not prove popular as the price of passage was not that much cheaper than the *Constitution* which continued to include full meals.

Nothing, not even the redesign to attract younger passengers, actually succeeded. Losing more and more money each year, American Export finally decided it could no longer run the ships. In September, 1968, the *Constitution* was sent to Jacksonville, Florida for an overhaul which never happened; she was moored in the harbor backwaters. Only three months later, a longshoreman's strike prevented provisioning her sister, the *Independence*. In spite of full booking in the early months of 1969, the company pulled the ship from service and mothballed her near Baltimore. Many passenger ships did not survive this low period in ocean cruising. The superliner, *United States*, was retired from service only a year later; within a few years, no American flag passenger ships operated out of New York.

CHAPTER SIX:
HAWAIIAN REBIRTH

From late 1968 to 1974, the *Constitution* and the *Independence* remained in lay up, one near Jacksonville, Florida, the other at Baltimore. Many foreign lines - Chandris, Lauro, and Home Lines - expressed interest in the ships. Chandris even tendered an offer, but nothing materialized. American Export discussed renewed Caribbean cruising with one or both of the vessels. An American group sought financing to acquire the ships, but the fuel crisis of 1973 made all lines wary of new acquisitions. The city of Jacksonville considered buying both ships for hotel and conference use, or even as a hospital. Both sat in their respective berths - lonely, sad, rusting.

In 1974, C.Y. Tung, the Chinese shipping magnate, acquired the two ships and reflagged them under Liberian registry. The following year, after a short refurbishment, Tung brought the *Independence* back into service as the *Oceanic Independence.* "The ship went directly from Baltimore to Durban in South Africa, where she made three cruises to the Indian Ocean," according to Luis Miguel Correia, a Portugese maritime author and historian. "These cruises were unsuccessful, however. She then found another charter, in the fall of 1975, for three roundtrip voyages between Walvis Bay in Angola and Lisbon. She carried 900 passengers to Lisbon on each trip. Angolan independence was coming that November, but already there were clashes and fighting. Many locals wanted to evacuate. And so, the South African Government chartered the *Oceanic Independence* for them. She would return empty to Walvis Bay and then after the last trip sailed out to Hong Kong." Thereafter, the *Oceanic Independence* stayed at anchor in Hong Kong. The *Constitution*

Matson Line
Ticket Pouch

did not sail at all in the 1970's and remained unchanged from when she had been towed to the Far East.

In 1977, the Tung group saw an opportunity for the *Oceanic Independence* to become a cruise ship, following a long tradition of liners serving Hawaii. Matson Line began service from San Francisco to Honolulu early in the twentieth century. The tradition of ocean travel to a Hawaiian paradise was, however, not enough; like other American lines, Matson suspended scheduled passenger service in 1970 in the face of increased fuel prices and declining passenger numbers.

Hawaii was, however, off limits for foreign lines. As American territory, Hawaiian navigation was defined by complex legislation from the 1930's known as the Jones Act. Its many clauses defined an "American" sailor and ship. American ships were solely those built in American shipyards, never flying a foreign flag. American sailors were American nationals. Only American ships, manned by American crews, could sail between American ports. Foreign ships might stop at a single American port en route to another country, but could never make two stops at American ports. This protectionist legislation was strongly supported by maritime unions, ship construction unions, and American lines. All of this meant that when Matson pulled out, no foreign line could take its place.

The new company, called American Hawaii Cruises, correctly saw that the Hawaiian cruise market was about to expand dramatically in the 1980's. Several factors made European destinations less attractive for Americans. The first was incidents of terrorism, especially the highjacking of aircraft. For example, in

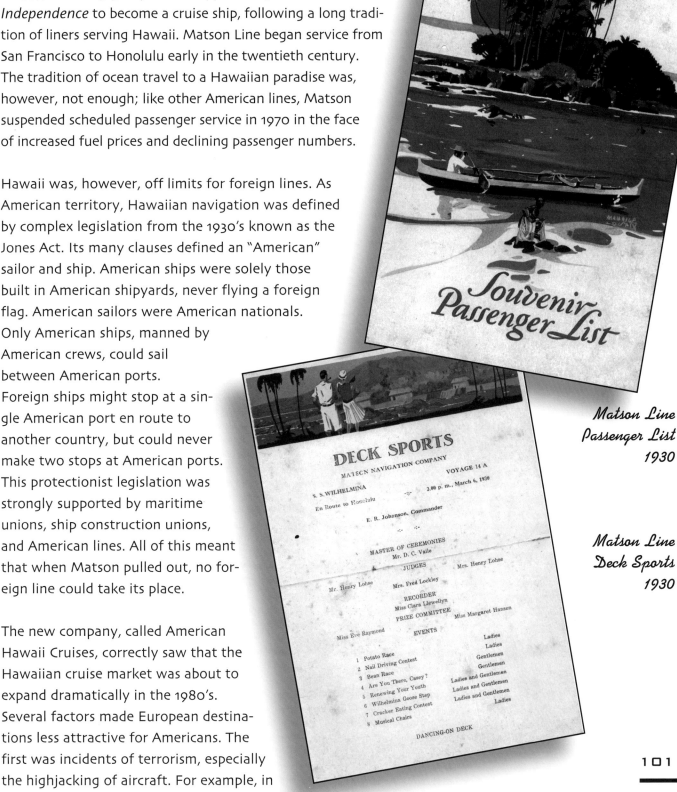

Matson Line
Passenger List
1930

Matson Line
Deck Sports
1930

Lounge, in the Design of the 1980s

the fall of 1977, terrorists took a Lufthansa flight on a 100 hour odyssey to Cyprus, Bahrain, Dubai, Aden, and Mogadishu (Somalia). There, a shootout with German commandos left all of the highjackers dead, but the passengers safe. Bombings and kidnappings in European cities originated with the IRA, Palestinians, radical Japanese and German groups, and Basque separatists. A more mundane factor discouraging European travel was the drop in the US dollar against European currencies, making European vacations more expensive. Finally, a generally conservative social and political drift (Ronald Reagan was already campaigning and would be elected in 1979) emphasized American loyalty and touring America. Hawaii was America's tropical paradise.

To these general factors must be added some specific to Hawaii. The State itself undertook a vigorous promotional campaign in the late 1970's which continued in the 1980's. Multipage ads appeared in *Time* magazine and other national periodicals. Probably more important was the stabilization of fuel prices after the rapid price increases by OPEC in 1973-74. New companies began to offer direct charter flights from America's heartland (Cleveland, St. Louis, Minneapolis, Detroit) to Hawaii. Simultaneously, bank deregulation allowed money to pour into hotel and resort development, much of it in Hawaii. Consumer awareness of Hawaii and its affordability arrived at the same time that new hotels and charter flights made it more available.

In spite of these advantages, the new company, American Hawaii, faced immediate obstacles to bringing the *Independence* back into service as a Hawaiian cruise ship. The same Jones Act which forbid foreign shipping in these waters also forbid any American ship which had carried a foreign flag. It would take an Act of Congress to exempt the *Independence* and allow her to be reflagged as an American vessel. The maritime unions, the ship fitting unions, and representatives from Hawaii aided the company in its lobbying efforts. Congress rewarded these lobbying efforts in 1979 with legislation which exempted the *Independence* from the reflagging restrictions of the Jones Act.

The Congressional success opened the way to financing, and work began immediately. Over several weeks, Coast Guard inspectors found the operating side of the ship in surprisingly good shape. To be sure, steel needed renewing, but not so much as to make the project financially unfeasible. Overall, the ship still benefited from the original overbuilding required by the government for potential wartime use. The ship, however, needed installation of a full complement of modern safety and navigation equipment. Bow thrusters were added for increased maneuverability in the smaller Hawaiian ports.

To refit the *Independence* for Hawaiian service, the ship also required complete interior refurbishing. She was given the colors and shades fashionable in hotel design in the period - shades of soft tan, grays, light wood, some chrome mixed with accent shades of mauve and blue. Recessed lighting predominated. The artwork reflected the color scheme of the rooms.

Lounge with Hawaiian Theme Mural, 1980s

Astronaut Scott Carpenter At The Relaunching of The Independence

All of this was
standard design for upscale hotels of
the era. In response to the ship's new environment,
workers removed room heaters and cut greater access to deck areas. The
plan added a show lounge for evening entertainment and an exercise center.

Then, additional problems arose from strict Coast Guard requirements for
fire safety. In some ways, the interior decoration was driven by the color of
fire resistant carpet available in time in the quantity needed. No passenger
ship had been refitted in American shipyards for so many years that most
carpet suppliers no longer made carpet capable of meeting Coast Guard
standards. Nevertheless, in six months, refitting was complete and the
Independence ready for her maiden voyage in Hawaii. On June 21, 1980,
Astronaut Scott Carpenter raised the American flag, bringing the
Independence back into American service.

Her earliest Hawiian service was a four-island, seven-day cruise, which remains the most popular package; American Hawaii marketed the ship as a comfortable way to see the islands without the bother of packing and unpacking or going to and from airports. The feel was that of a hotel with small touches of Hawaii - some local entertainment, some Hawaiian food, and a bit of Hawaiian artwork. Shore excursions to spectacular tropical sites were the "stars" of these cruises.

In 1980-81, the *Independence* booked 25,000 passengers on forty cruises, yielding a promising occupancy rate of just under 80 per cent. With this favorable response, American Hawaii decided to refurbish the *Constitution* for similar service. A second round of lobbying Congress for an exemption from the Jones Act was easier; the special bill was signed by President Reagan in 1982.

On Board Entertainment

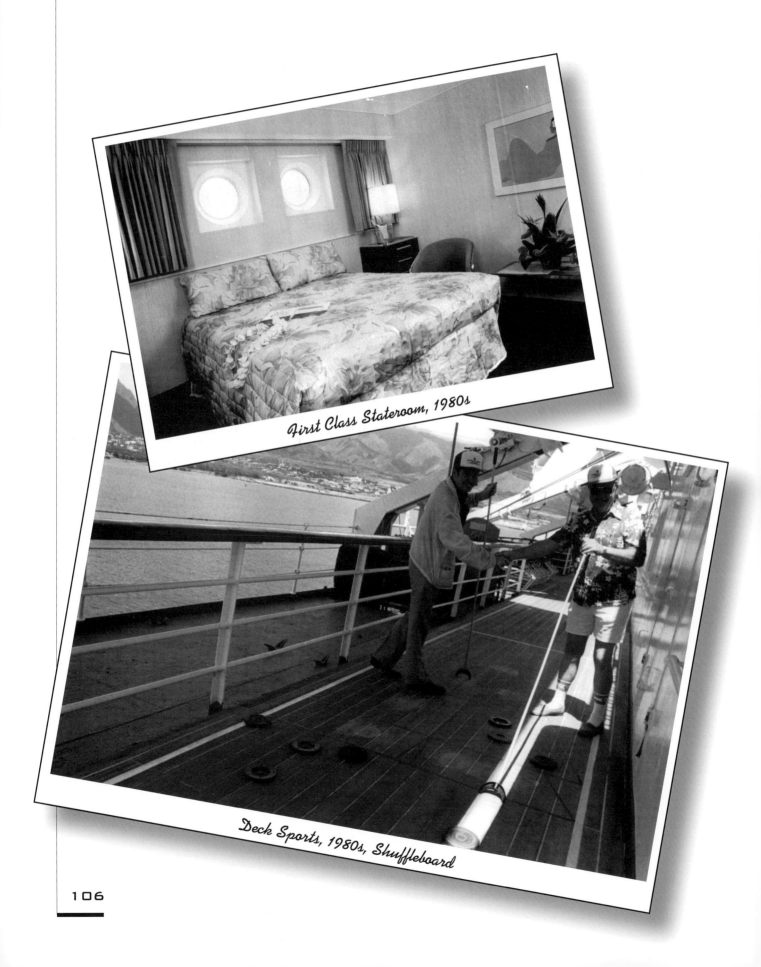

First Class Stateroom, 1980s

Deck Sports, 1980s, Shuffleboard

Hawaiian Entertainment

Hawaiian Dancers

Cruising Hawaii

On the whole, the *Constitution* was in worse shape than the *Independence* had been. While the *Independence* had sailed and been maintained in the 1970's, the *Constitution* had not. She had been in layup in Jacksonville and then in Hong Kong. Inspection revealed, for example, that 250 tons of steel would have to be renewed, 4000 tubes replaced in the ship's four boilers, and a modern sewage disposal system installed. As with the *Independence*, renovation plans called for bow thrusters, a modern navigation system, an additional stairway, and more openings to the decks. The complete design of the interior was easier than for the *Independence*, as designers had already located sources for fire retardant fabrics and carpet. Also, licensing agencies had upgraded hotel fire regulations in the time between the sister ships' renovations, so that many manufacturers had generated new products to meet the regulations.

After more than a year of work, re-christening of the of the ship re-united Princess Grace of Monaco and the *Constitution*. She and Prince Rainier were traveling in the Far East and agreed to come to a shipyard at Kaohsiung on Taiwan for the occasion. Grace's short speech suggests her affection for the ship.

Constitution, a name close to my heart, for just over twenty five years ago I crossed the Atlantic on my way from my home in America for my marriage and new life in the Principality of Monaco. Now the great ship will link up the Hawaiian Islands in a chain bringing together both sides of another ocean - the Pacific. May she sail in peace, safety and prosperity, and may God bless her and all who sail in her.

Tragically, only five months later, Princess Grace died in a car accident in Monaco.

On Board Memorial Wreath for Grace Kelly

Through the 1980's, the sister ships carried more than a million passengers - families, retirees, honeymooners. Most were vacationers, enjoying the beauty of Hawaii and the warmth of tropical seas. Some were famous. Cary Grant with his wife and daughter returned to the ship which figured so prominently in his famous film, *An Affair to Remember*. The *Constitution* also "starred" in a sequence of *Magnum P.I.*, starring Tom Selleck.

Cary Grant, His Wfe and Daughter, Sail The Constitution

Tom Selleck and The Cast of "Magnum, P.J."

Tom Selleck With Captain T. Y. Wu

Jonathan Winters Clowns with a Crew Member

Young Dancers On Deck

"I Dream Of Jeannie" Star Barbara Eden On Board

Welcoming Bob Hope for a Cruise

The Constitution Off The Kauai Coast

CHAPTER SEVEN:
THE SHIPS TODAY

115

At the opening of the 1990's, in spite of promising occupancy rates, the ships were not showing a profit. Two American insurance companies that had financed Tung's original acquisition of the ships brought in a new corporate team headed by Peter Huang (from the securities field), but the new team could not reverse larger trends. The original Hawaii tourist boom had cooled; excess hotel building in the 1980's on the islands resulted in discounted rates for both rooms and cabins. Further, American Hawaii was saddled with the debt of a failed Hawaii-Tahiti service which the company had inaugurated in 1986. Finally, in 1992, a major hurricane flattened Kauai, one of the ship's most desirable stops. The company could afford neither major repairs which safety regulations required nor a major restyling to stay competitive with other hotels and resorts in Hawaii. Sam Zell, American entrepreneur and real estate investor, acquired the ships in early 1993, through a negotiated settlement with the two insurance companies. Thus the ships returned to true American ownership.

Hotel Area, Renovation of 1994

Conversion of Athletic Club to Cabins, 1994

The Zell group knew that both ships would need full refurbishment and
redesign in addition to mechanical work. They began with the *Independence*.
To head the design team, American Hawaii tapped Al Luthmers, an architect
fresh from the redesign of the Delta Queen Steamboat Company's riverboats
and the construction of an extraordinary new riverboat, the *American Queen*.
In April 1993, Luthmers took the first of many trips aboard the *Independence*.
His design notes show that from his first encounter he was impressed by
the ship itself. "The steel is fabulous. All the ship detail is great: the big deck,
the railings, the cascading balconies, the stacks, the canted windows; it is a
very convincing piece of work". He sought to change things which were
"inconsistent with the dignity and power of this wonderful old boat."

Shrouded Funnels, Work In Progress, 1994

"It was designed by Henry Dreyfuss, a ... greatly respected industrial designer who did interiors on many of the great trains. It turns out that everything I like about this boat , especially the exterior, is on purpose. It is important that we locate as much original material about what this boat was back in 1951 as we can as a frame of reference for understanding what to do going forward. It was interesting to learn that all the confusion in the elevators ...is a result of the fact that this boat was originally three classes and that they were completely separate from one another - this explains why some elevators go some places and not others, etc. This is a tremendous advantage to have the original concept down through design detail, having been crafted by a good designer. The night lights, the door hardware, the vent holes in the closet, the beautifully detailed interior stairways, the cascade of the aft decks; I am so pleased that our basic material is this good."

"The semi-circular bar at the aft end of the Promenade deck is a very clean, straightforward functional space where the geometry, the windows and the purpose seem to work easily together."

"The aft end of the Sun Deck is an absolutely gorgeous situation. It overlooks the cascade of wood decks past the Promenade Deck to the grand open deck on the Upper Deck level with its swimming pool. The swimming pool portion of the deck has a generous surround for chaise lounges and it is framed by two extraordinary tongue-like extended balcony decks on the level above."

Overall, the initial design surveys arrived at two themes. One would emphasize the triumph of Henry Dreyfuss' design; the other would be to make the ship truly Hawaiian by opening the ship to the tropical environment and featuring Hawaiian culture. Again, quoting from the design notes of Al Luthmers:

Work On Decks, 1994

"...the only way to keep people coming to Hawaii is its "Hawaii-ness". The point was made that tropical landscapes and lush sand beaches are abundantly available on the planet and most places they are much cheaper to get to and enjoy so the big draw here is cultural, the historic island culture. The great enemy is fake Hawaii culture, the degrading and exploiting of Hawaii's special qualities and integrity in cheap stereotypical ways - t-shirt shops, junky souvenirs."

These two themes - the integrity of Henry Dreyfuss' original design and the experience of authentic Hawaiian culture - would become the touchstones of the major renovation during the six-month drydock of 1994.

The repairs began on July 5, when the *Independence* left service in Hawaii. All the way across the Pacific and through the Panama Canal, a crew worked on non-essential systems, removed asbestos, and did necessary demolition. When the *Independence* reached drydock at Newport News, Virginia, there remained several thousand repairs required by the operation of the ship - from chipping and painting all the deck rail supports to replacing the sewage treatment system and renewing tons of steel throughout the ship. The plan called for new cabins and suites on all of the upper decks, a new retail space, upgrades of existing cabins, new carpeting and lighting in the corridors, and

Drydock, 1994

major work on the public areas. After dock and sea trials, work continued throughout the return voyage, chipping and painting right through the time of the first scheduled cruise in October. (Construction delays forced the cancellation of five cruises in October and November.)

Three main areas were altered during this dry-dock. New cabins were added on the upper decks. A large buffet was built in the center of the main deck and attached to the aft open areas by larger doors. Perhaps the most striking change was the configuration of the Kama'aina Lounge. Even during service in Hawaii, this lounge had remained enclosed. The lanais (side galleries) were closed off, locked, and separated from the lounge by heavy drapes. The windowed galleries were designated life boat stations and were required to remain empty. By changing from life boats to life rafts, these two wonderful galleries became available for passenger use. New open doors joined the lanais to the lounge with the windows in the lanais open to the tropical warmth. With wicker furniture and plants, these have become one of the most popular and appreciated areas of the ship.

Through The Panama Canal, Work Goes On

The other main change was one of ethos. Management decided that the experience of Hawaii should permeate the ship. They brought on board a "kumu", a spiritual elder, deeply immersed in Hawaiian culture. She lectures, points out sights, teaches music and other aspects of the culture. Hawaiian dancing and music are also featured in the daily entertainment. Hawaiian artwork, flowers, plants, and wall coverings are found throughout the ship. Hawaiian foods show up often on the menu; several movies set in Hawaii are screened on each cruise.

The considerable cost of renovating the *Independence* made it no longer financially feasible to renovate the *Constitution*. The ship stayed in service until the summer of 1995, when she sailed to a shipyard at Portland, Oregon. Various plans were discussed, including conversion to a floating university,

Passengers Make Leis in the Lanai

Kama'aina Lounge, Completed

housing for the Navy, and sale for use as a gambling ship. The *Constitution* was, however, finally sold for scrap in October, 1997. This mighty ship, the pride of America's technical prowess after World War II, this product of Cold War politics, this playground for the rich and gateway for the humble, this beautiful ship for the beautiful Grace Kelly sank in the Pacific northeast of Hawaii on November 17, 1997, while in tow to an Asian scrap yard. She will rest forever on the floor of the Pacific Ocean.

The *Independence*, however, continues to bring joy to approximately 50,000 passengers every year. The ship serves as floating hotel, cruise ship, and site for cultural events for its passengers. They not only have the chance to experience the tropical charm of Hawaii; they enjoy it from the decks of one of the few classic American liners still afloat. The design of Henry Dreyfuss is as modern today as when the ship was built more than fifty years ago. Long may the *Independence* sail in her Hawaiian setting.

Cruising With the Windows Open

Rattan, Palms, and Tropical Breezes

The Cascade of the Rear Decks

Completed Conversion Of Athletic Club to Cabins

Lei Making, Starboard Lanai

Cruising the Green Isles

The Kama'aina Lounge

Honolulu Harbor

The Romance of Hawaii

During her first days in commercial service in Februrary 1951, the *Independence* steamed eastwards across the mid-Atlantic on the 6-day passage to her first port of call, Funchal, on the island of Madeira. Frank Braynard wrote a piece for the *Herald Tribune* which considered the question of just how big the *Independence* was. The article was entitled "Four Yardsticks Give Four Sizes to *Independence*."

"Four major tonnage measurement systems in use today make a comparison of ship tonnages indecisive unless reached under the same yardstick. The brand new *Independence* is a case in point. The liner has been advertised and generally described as being a ship of 26,000 gross tons. Final determination of her actual measurement, however, showed that she might be classed anywhere from 23,000 to 30,000 gross tons, depending on which of the four judging categories are used. At Quincy and finally at Boston, more than a year was required to measure her, a laborious determination of cubical content by tape and yardstick in every included area throughout the 683 foot vessel. James G. Hartigan, chief measurer of vessels at the Custom House, Boston, headed a staff of technicians who walked, wriggled and crawled through every compartment in the vessel as her hull rose from the slipway."

According to Braynard's findings, the *Independence* is a vessel of 23,719 gross tons under American rules of measurement. By British rules, the new liner was classed as 29,496 gross tons. By Panama Canal rules, the *Independence* is a ship of 29,965 gross tons, but by the rules in force at the Suez Canal, the liner measures 30,105 gross tons. The chief difference between the British and the American measurement systems is that under British rules the ship's entire superstructure is counted while only the cubic content of the hull and the first deck attached directly to the hull are measured by the Americans. A gross ton is 100 cubic feet of permanently enclosed space under both systems, however. Braynard concluded, "By using the British system, the *Independence* becomes the tenth largest ship in the world. The *America*, largest US-flag passenger liner, is measured as of 26,314 gross tons by American standards, but becomes 33,532 gross tons under British measurement. The new United States Lines' superliner [the *United States*] will measure about 48,000 tons under the American system, but should be at least 60,000 gross tons under British measurement rules."

SUNLIGHT & STEEL: ACKNOWLEDGEMENTS

Within American Hawaii Cruises, current owners of the *Independence*, many have gone out of their way to assist this project. These include, in Hawaii, Jim Nobles, who started the project and gave it his support at crucial times; in Chicago, John Rau gave his time, knowledge of Henry Dreyfuss, and photos; Deborah Contraris made available construction photos, let us loose in the mass of old files on the ships, and talked about the 1994 lay up; Phil Calian found time to discuss acquisition of the ships. From Oregon, Al Luthmers shared thoughts about design work on the ships in 1994 and 1996.

We wish to thank the *AAA Motor News* and *Cruise Travel* for printing authors' requests which located several people who had worked and traveled on the ships.

The following, from their affection for the ships, provided interviews of their experiences with them:

Norton Bain	Joseph Kowalski
Everett Viez	Claudia Lonzetti
Frank Braynard	Herb Maletz
Gus de Chelle	Reverand Neville Rucker
Maria Cuocci	Der Scutt
John Dapper	Michael Shernoff
Richard Faber	John Todd
Lew Gordon	Jack Weatherford
Carla Kimble	

SUNLIGHT & STEEL:
SOURCES

CHAPTER ONE: THE PRINCESS AND THE PRINCE

The Daily Worker, January-June, 1956.

Steven Englund, Grace of Monaco (Garden City, New Jersey, 1984).

Bob Harrow, interview, 1997.

Robert Lacey, Grace (New York, 1994).

Life, January-June, 1956.

Judith Balaban Quine, The Bridesmaids (New York, 1989).

Jeffery Robinson, Rainier and Grace (New York, 1989).

Time, January-June, 1956.

Womenswear Daily, January-June, 1956.

OTHER SOURCES

N.R.P. Bonsor, North Atlantic Seaway (Prescott, England, 1955).

George Devol (ed.), Ocean and Cruise News, (Stamford, Connecticut, 1980-97).

Henry Dreyfuss, Designing for People (New York, 1955).

Peter Eisele & William Rau (eds.), Steamboat Bill (New York, New York, 1966-97).

Allen E. Jordan, Saluting the Aloha Spirit: American Hawaii's First Decade (Lausanne, Switzerland, 1990).

Arnold Kludas, Great Passenger Ships of the World Today (Sparkford, England, 1992).

William Miller, The Cruiseships (London, England, 1988).

William Miller, The Last Atlantic Liners (London, England, 1985).

William Miller, Transatlantic Liners 1945-80 (Newton Abbot, England, 1981).

L.A. Sawyer & W.H. Mitchell, From America to United States (Kendal, England, 1979-86).

SUNLIGHT & STEEL: ILLUSTRATION CREDITS

American Hawaii Cruises, pg. 29 (upper) -39, 43-50, 54-55, 64-65, 74, 99, 102-108, 110-113, 115, 121-126

I. U. DeChellis, pg. 85 (upper), 88

Henry Dreyfuss, <u>Designing for People</u> (New York, 1955) pg. 35 (telephones), 52, 90

Stewart Gordon, pg. 57, 63, 76-77, 85-87, 89, 100-101

Bob Harrow, pg. 1-16, 53, 66-71, 78-80, 84, 90 (lower), 91-92

Claudia Lonzetti, pg. 61 (lower), 72-73

MIT Museum, Hart Nautical Collection, Pg. 40-42

William Miller, pg. 19-27, 37 (lower), 84 (lower), 96

Newport News Shipbuilding, 116-120

John Rau, pg. 29 (lower), 56, 58, 61, 75, 83, 90, 93-94, 109

John Todd, pg. 51, 92 (lower)

Stewart Gordon

is an historian specializing both in American popular culture and in India. He has been historical consultant and provided antique furnishings and artwork for more than thirty hotel projects, including the Grand Floridian Hotel at Disneyworld and all three riverboats belonging to the Delta Queen Steamboat Company. He served as historical consultant for the *Independence* in 1995-96. He currently teaches history at the University of Michigan and lives with his wife, Sara, in Ann Arbor.

William Miller

is one of the world's authorities on ocean liners. He has written more than forty books - from books on individual lines to wartime use of ocean liners - and more than 750 articles. He travels the world's passenger ships regularly, as lecturer and reviewer, and has logged more than 200 voyages. He has appeared in several TV documentaries about liners and is active in societies and museums of maritime history. He lives in Secaucus, New Jersey.

Bob Harrow

Recently retired, Bob was a photojournalist and pioneer of onboard photography. He was aboard the *Independence* and the *Constitution* in the 1950's and 1960's. His firm, Transocean Photo, led by his sons, is one of the largest onboard photographic services in the world.

Joseph Radding

is an art director, graphic designer, and illustrator. He lives with his wife Marilee in Ann Arbor, Michigan.

You may order this book by sending a check or money order for $22.95 to:

> Prow Press
> Box 4190
> Ann Arbor, MI 48105

If you enjoyed "Sunlight and Steel", you might like another publication of Prow Press entitled "Our Vacation: A 1910 Riverboat Adventure." This book is based on an album of historical photographs. Two brothers and their wives rode the *City of Savannah*, a Mark Twain-style paddle wheel packet, from St. Louis all the way south to Florence, Mississippi. Their early amateur photos capture loading cattle and unloading freight, casting the lead, as well as their fellow passengers, the captain and crew, and all of the towns along the way. Along the way we learn the history of the family and the towns and much riverboat lore.

If you would like to receive information about this and other upcoming Prow Press publications, please send your name and mailing address to the address listed above.

Stewart Gordon may be contacted by e-mail at gordonstu@aol.com